LOVE REMEMBERED

When in disgrace with Fortune and men's eyes
I all alone beweep my outcast state,
And trouble deaf heaven with my bootless cries,
And look upon myself and curse my fate,
Wishing me like to one more rich in hope,
Featured like him, like him with friends possessed,
Desiring this man's art, and that man's scope,
With what I most enjoy contented least,
Yet in these thoughts my self almost despising,
Haply I think on thee, and then my state,
(Like to the lark at break of day arising
From sullen earth) sings hymns at heaven's gate,
For thy sweet love remembered such wealth brings,
That then I scorn to change my state with kings.

William Shakespeare

Peter Hannan SJ

Love Remembered
THE MEANING AND BEAUTY OF THE MASS

the columba press

First published in 2005 by
the columba press
55A Spruce Avenue, Stillorgan Industrial Park,
Blackrock, Co Dublin

Cover by Bill Bolger
Origination by The Columba Press
Printed in Ireland by ColourBooks Ltd, Dublin

ISBN 1 85607 493 5

Acknowledgements

I wish to express my gratitude to all those who over the years have contributed to making the Mass what it means to me today. I want to remember those who risked their lives in times of persecution to keep the Mass alive among us. I want to thank my parents, my family, my friends and the various Jesuit communities in which I have lived who have passed on to me their own deep understanding and appreciation of the Mass. For the huge contribution Genevieve Tobin has made to this book I am deeply grateful, for her enthusiasm, her expert advice, her eye for detail and for the hours of hard work she devoted to it.

Table of Contents

Introduction

I was at a boarding school for nine years around the time of the Second World War. At that time, life in such an institution was spartan, the food was basic and the heating system was poor. It was a harsh environment to grow up in but it was made tolerable by the companionship that developed among those of us who went through the experience together.

Leaving home at the beginning of each term was hard but it was almost worth it for the joy I experienced as the terms came to an end and I returned to the warm environment of home. There I had a renewed sense of how well my father provided for us in creating an atmosphere of security. My six brothers and especially my three sisters made me feel cared for and significant in a way I did not initially experience at school. But it was the delight in my mother's eyes when I arrived home on holidays which almost made the going away worthwhile. The meals she prepared, the warm atmosphere of home she cultivated and especially the joy of her presence were some of the things I appreciated all the more because of the harsh environment I experienced in the boarding school.

At the end of the holidays, especially at the end of the long Summer ones, I was built up and ready to return to school again. The pain of leaving home was eased by the prospect of escaping the hard work of harvest time but mainly by the prospect of meeting again the friends I was making at school. These deepening relationships with the boys I was with in class each day, played football with, and shared my young dreams with, expanded the environment I experienced at home in new and challenging ways. Bonds formed with some of my new found friends that have lasted a lifetime. These friendships provided in my formative years a basic experience of something I longed for then and continue to long for. This is an experience of being

loved or, in more concrete terms, of being accepted and appreciated, cared for and acknowledged as significant. These friends,
along with my family, created a caring environment I felt at
home in, a place where I felt secure because within its bound-
aries I felt loved.

Two characteristics of our environment
One of the characteristics of this caring environment which is so
important for us throughout our lives is the need to leave it and
another characteristic is our need to return to it. We need to
leave its caring atmosphere if we are to broaden and deepen the
relationships within which we experience its care. We also need
to return to those who have cared for us if we are to be sustained
by them. We need to reach out towards all the love that is yet to
be, as well as to rest in the love we have received. If we are to answer the call of the gospel to believe that we are God's beloved
we need to cultivate this vision of ourselves as well as leave behind old ways of seeing ourselves that are at variance with this
vision. This desire to call ourselves 'beloved on the earth' inspires life's fundamental quest to 'repent and believe the
gospel'. (Mk 1:14-15)

> And did you get what
> You wanted from life, even so?
> I did
> And what did you want?
> To call myself beloved, to feel myself
> beloved on the earth.
> *(Raymond Carver)*

This desire to 'feel myself beloved on the earth' can never be
fully satisfied by human love which is of its nature limited and
often falls short of what we long for. We are made for a love that
is not limited and our hearts will be restless till we find and rest
in a love that only God can supply. This search becomes a realistic one when Jesus reveals that we are loved by him and his
Father as they love each other. (Jn 17:23) The fact that only this
love will satisfy us is the point of the legend of the Holy Grail in

its portrayal of life as a journey in search of the love of Jesus, of its extent, its depth and its passionate intensity. On this journey we are constantly leaving lesser loves behind in order to find this the greatest and most comprehensive of loves the world has ever known. (Jn 15:13) In the Grail legend this love is symbolised by the cup and plate used by Jesus at the Last Supper and by the bread and wine at every Mass.

The importance of these two movements in life by which we are constantly drawn – to leave our caring environment but also to return to it – are very powerfully illustrated for us in the film *Cinema Paradiso.*

The film tells the story of Toto who is a well known Italian film director. It covers two periods in his life, one when he is growing up in Sicily and living with his mother and sister. His father had died in the second world war. The second period covers a few days 30 years later when he returns home for a funeral.

There are four powerful influences in Toto's life. There is the environment his mother provides for him and that which Alfredo the projectionist at the local cinema provides. There is the influence of Elena, the girl he falls in love with as a teenager, and the influence of the cinema.

While his mother is prominent in Toto's early life, her influence on him only emerges when, after an absence of 30 years, he returns home for Alfredo's funeral. While Toto had been away she had set aside a room in her house where she had put all the things associated with the story of his life as a boy and as a young man. When he returns home we see how beautiful is her concern for him, in its deference and wisdom. While not wanting to interfere in his affairs she gives him the gift of the wisdom she has learned from life.

Elena has remained the love of his life but a set of tragic circumstances has kept them apart. Both of them have felt that the other failed to be true to the love they pledged each other, but they are reconciled when they meet again in a very moving scene in the film. However, they both now realise that they must travel on apart from each other as she has committed herself so someone else. He realises that in every woman he has met it was Elena he had been looking for but that now he must be content to live with the memory of her love and move on.

Alfredo represents the masculine side of the environment in which Toto has grown up and is more than a father to him. He is conscious of Toto's potential and he sees that if Toto is to realise his dream he must leave Sicily. So where his mother gave Toto roots, Alfredo gave him wings in the belief that the small town in which they lived would confine and even suffocate his talent.

The fourth influence that formed the environment in which Toto grew up was the local cinema. There, people are enticed into reflecting on their lives in the light of the traditional wisdom expressed in the stories that unfold before them. The films engage them and put them in touch with their dream of romantic love and the bliss it promises. The cinema is aptly called Cinema Paradiso because in it, for a brief spell, their dream of a loving environment, where they find the happiness for which they crave, is realised. They all know that the love they experience in their own lives is much more limited than that portrayed in the films. Nevertheless, they enjoy the time the films offer them to be with the love and the bliss they dream of. In the light of this, the final scene of the film is particularly significant. In it we see Toto, who now spends his life making films, enjoying Alfredo's final bequest to him. This is a series of scenes from various films where the hero and heroine embrace in that moment of romantic love at the climax of the film.

The Toto we now see enjoying these romantic scenes is a much happier person than the one who flew home for Alfredo's funeral. We are left to wonder at the effect on him of having returned home where he touched again and was in turn touched by those who loved him. Is it this love and the environment it creates that sets him free from the illusion of romantic love and its false promises? Is he now free to live in a more realistic and contented way, conscious of all the love he has received?

Care makes and sustains us

There is a very significant Greek story that is all the more so for being pre-Christian. It is a story about Care who one day moulded a figure out of clay and called it a human being. When she asked Jupiter to give life to what she had formed he agreed on condition that it be called after him. Care was not happy with this condition that Jupiter set down so they decided that they would ask Saturn to decide what they should do. After pondering the matter Saturn decided that there were three parties who had a claim to what Care had moulded. Since it was made out of clay then it should return to the earth when it died. If Jupiter gave it life then at death its spirit or life should return to him. However, as long as it lived it should belong to Care and be called after her as she was the one who had created it and would sustain it as long as it lived.

The holding environment

Each of us needs to develop and maintain a place in life within which we can keep in touch with Care, for it is she who constantly creates or expands our life, as well as sustains it. What Care creates and sustains is called 'the holding environment' by the Canadian psychoanalyst Donald Winnicott. He describes it in the following way:

> The holding environment includes the whole routine of care throughout the day and night, and is not the same with any two infants because it is part of the infant and no two infants are alike. Also, it follows the minute day-to-day changes belonging to the infant's growth and development, both physical and psychological.

What Winnicott refers to as 'the holding environment' are the circumstances we need as infants if we are to grow. Chief among these is the way we are held by our mother as she provides surroundings for us which are like those her womb provided for us before birth. These caring circumstances, which the child needs if he or she is to develop, are similar to those of a seedling. There is a stage after a seedling is germinated when it is very fragile so that its life depends on the provision of just the right amount of light, warmth and moisture. A deficiency in any of these basic requirements will mean that the plant fails to mature properly. If the seedling is provided with the right environment it becomes much more capable as a plant of coping with the harsher conditions outside the glasshouse. Even though as a plant it is less exacting of the care it requires as a seedling, it always requires a healthy environment if it is to realise all its potential.

Qualities of a good holding environment
In his book *Facets of Unity*, A. H. Almaas uses Winnicott's image of the holding environment and describes some of the qualities it needs to have:

> A good holding environment is all that is needed for the human soul to grow and develop into what she can become. It needs to provide a sense of safety and security, the sense that you are, and can count on, being taken care of. Your soul needs an environment that is dependable, consistent, attuned to your needs, and that provides for you in a way that is empathic to these needs. This is the ideal environment for human growth. If the environment has a good sense of holding, you will experience basic trust ... and confidence in reality.

Even though people become more and more independent as they move from infancy to childhood and from adolescence to adult life they still need to feel secure, significant and cared for. This not only sustains them but helps them to develop as well. More specifically the caring environment we always need if we are to mature is one where we experience four basic kinds of care. We need to be *acknowledged* as significant, to be *accepted* as limited and sinful, to be *appreciated* as predominantly good, and to have our basic needs *cared for*.

Building up our holding environment

As an infant the care that makes and sustains us is taken in at the sensate levels of touch, taste and smell as well as through what we see and hear. As we move out of infancy our feelings begin to play an important role in our relationships. When we become adults the glimpses we get of ourselves as cared for, from the way people look at or treat us, become vitally important. These glimpses, if articulated, dwelt with and owned, can become convictions. These convictions are the foundation on which our holding environment is built.

There are two sources of these convictions that we need to keep in touch with. One of these, which we might call the human source, consists in the people in our lives who care for us and ask us to believe that they do. The other source, which we might call the divine source, consists in the good news of God's love and providence that Jesus and the Holy Spirit foster our belief in. The story of the revelation of this love is told in the Word of God but it is in the death and resurrection of Jesus that it finds its fullest expression. Of this love Jesus says, 'No one can have greater love than to lay down one's life for one's friends.' (Jn 15:13) It is this supreme expression of love and the environment it creates that the Mass seeks to remember and thus renew.

This environment which Mass seeks to sustain is one in which God's love pervades. It is in us and all around us in everything that makes up this environment. We find this belief expressed in Psalm 139, in the first article of the Nicene Creed we say at Mass, and in the Celtic image of the lorica. The lorica is a leather jacket people used long ago, not just to keep them warm, but to shield them from attack. It had the same function as a breastplate but it fitted more closely and was more flexible in accommodating itself to the shape and movement of the body. In the Celtic worldview, the lorica is a favourite image of God's providence in prayers like the breastplate of St Patrick and in the 7th century Lorica of St Fursa.

The Lorica of St Fursa
The arm of God be around my shoulders,
the touch of the Holy Spirit upon my head,
the sign of Christ's cross be upon my forehead,
the sound of the Holy Spirit in my ears,
the fragrance of the Holy Spirit in my nostrils,
the vision of heaven's company in my eyes,
the conversation of heaven's company on my lips,
the work of God's church in my hands,
the service of God and the neighbour in my feet,
a home for God in my heart,
and to God, the Father of all, my entire being. Amen

Why do we forget?
Though we long to return to the environment in which we find
life and happiness we have great difficulty in doing so. There are
two reasons for this. The first is that once we begin to dwell on
the story of our holding environment we are likely to come face
to face with painful aspects of it. The sources of this pain are the
deficiencies of the environment in which we grew up. These are
likely to surface as soon as we reflect on our story. This is a feature of the holding environment that Winnicott noticed when he
observed that infants become conscious of their holding environment only when it is deficient.

> ... it is when things do not go well that the infant becomes
> aware, not of the failure of maternal care, but of the results,
> whatever they may be, of that failure; that is to say, the infant
> becomes aware of reacting to some impingement.

These deficiencies may be only a small part of the whole picture
of the circumstances in which we grew up, but the tendency to
become fixated with this five per cent or so of our experience is a
tendency that endures throughout life.

Another reason why we may not want to return to the care
which makes and sustains us is the effort involved in doing so.
We are reluctant, in lives that are already overcrowded, to make

the space required for this kind of reflection. Making this space will involve the time, the energy and the resources needed to become aware of the people and events which have been instrumental in the growth of our sense of being cared for. Once we have noticed some aspect of the care that sustains us, believing in this 'good news' involves 'repentance' or a difficult change of mind and heart. This for most people is more trouble than it is worth.

If we fail to cultivate our holding environment it becomes dormant and then we live with a level of love that, though it sustains life, it is not the abundance of life and happiness Jesus comes to share with us. (Jn 10:10, Jn 15:11) Rather than entering the banquet that symbolises this abundance we choose to survive on a subsistence diet. (Mt 22:1-14)

The effect of forgetting
There is a saying in the book of Wisdom which captures the effect of allowing ourselves to forget the abundance of the 'kindness' God surrounds us with and the holding environment this creates:

> ... by sinking into deep forgetfulness they get cut off from your kindness. No herb, no poultice cured them, but it was your word, Lord, which heals all things. (Wis 16:11-12)

When we allow ourselves to forget all the kindness shown to us during our lives and the healthy environment this could create for us, something very damaging happens. There is a striking example of this in chapters 3-12 of the book of Genesis. When the people separated themselves from God, and the love God essentially is, they found that their relationships with themselves, with others and with the whole of creation disintegrated. As a result the environment in which they lived became a hostile rather than a holding one.

In these circumstances, where people are no longer willing to keep in touch with the love they have received and the worth this gives them, they seek to earn their own worth. For example they seek to earn a sense of significance through the work they do or through the wealth they accumulate. However, what sense of worth they earn through what they have or what they do is limited, fleeting and fragile. Because what they earn in this way is such an impoverished version of what God has made them for, feelings like frustration, guilt, anxiety and sadness become prevalent. They find themselves in a competitive environment where they are only as good as their last job. In these circumstances their security and significance are constantly questioned.

Love remembered and an environment renewed
It is in circumstances like these that we can appreciate the role of Mass in renewing our environment. It renews our experience of the intensity of Jesus' love when he sacrifices his life for each of us. At every Mass we are invited to say with Paul, 'the life I now live in the flesh I live by faith in the Son of God, who loved me and gave himself for me.' (Gal 2:20) Where the environment we build out of our own resources is fragile, fleeting and superficial, the one that the Mass keeps us in touch with is rock-like, permanent and profound. This is because the love this environment is built on is the greatest love that exists.

> No one has greater love than this, to lay down one's life for one's friends. (Jn 15:13)

Thus the Mass provides us with a powerful way of renewing our vision of Jesus' love and the environment it creates. It also provides us with a way of making our own of this vision when Jesus invites us to 'eat' his body 'given for' us and to 'drink' his blood 'poured out for' us. (Lk 22:19-20) By eating his body and drinking his blood we not only assimilate his love but we build up the extraordinarily intimate environment in which we abide in him and he in us.

> Those who eat my flesh and drink my blood abide in me, and I in them. (Jn 6:56)

An outline of the five parts of this book

In this introduction so far we have looked at the vision of love the Mass seeks to renew and how this love creates and sustains an environment in which we can live life to the full. (Jn 10:10) In the five parts of this book we will examine five aspects of this love that the Mass seeks to remember and renew.

- In the first part we will examine the Mass as a way of renewing the vision of God's love that Jesus reveals to us.

- In the second part we will look at different aspects of this love and at the role the Word of God and our personal experience play in revealing it.

- In the third part we will reflect on how we immerse our whole person in the love revealed to us at Mass.

- In the fourth part we will consider how immersing ourselves in Jesus' love can transform the whole environment in which we live by reintegrating all our relationships.

- In the fifth part we will focus on the qualities of this reintegrated environment that we seek to renew in the communion of the Mass.

Each of the five parts is preceded by a story which illustrates the theme of the part it precedes. At the beginning of each chapter there will be a brief reflection on some aspect of this story. It is hoped that this will make the theme of each chapter more engaging.

There will be some suggestions for reflection and prayer at the end of each chapter. These are meant to provide an opportunity to experience the ideas put forward in the chapter in a more personal and experiential way. It is hoped that these suggestions will help to convert the theoretical and exterior knowledge that the body of the chapter provides into a more practical and interior knowledge. For the exercises to be effective it is important to write out the reflections that the exercises invite you to make.

PART 1

Remembering the love that sustains us

Part 1 examines the vision of Jesus' love which the Mass renews, and the response this vision calls for.

Chapter 1 invites us to consider whether the Mass is primarily Grace, or something God wants to do for us, or is it primarily worship, or something we do for God.

Chapter 2 looks at four aspects of Grace and how these provide a context for understanding the Mass.

Behind the Sun

The film *Behind the Sun* tells the story of a Brazilian family who live on a farm from which they barely eke out a living. Their world is dominated by unrelenting work and by the violence of a feud that is going on between themselves and a family who live on a neighbouring farm. As the film begins we are introduced to the latest episode in this feud. The bloodstained shirt of the eldest son is hung on a line outside their house and when the blood on it turns yellow the second son will have to set out to kill a son of the family on the neighbouring farm. So we are caught up in a story which, as the mother says, 'is dominated by the dead'. The violence of these killings infects their whole lives.

The father rules his wife and the two remaining sons with an iron fist. We see an example of this when the youngest son, a lad of ten or so, suggests that his brother should not have to continue this cycle of violence. He is knocked off his chair with a slap across the face by his father. This violence affects their work too as the father drives his family in their task of extracting sugar from the cane they grow on their farm. Even the oxen who drive the sugar extracting machine are beaten mercilessly by the father.

It is in this harsh environment that the youngest son, called Poko, and his brother seek to create another world that is dominated by the care they have for each other. This caring environment is deeply influenced early on in the story when Poko is given a book of folk tales. One of these stories about a mermaid captures his imagination. Any spare time he has is spent sitting under a tree in front of their house telling himself this story. In this way Poko re-enacts his dream about journeying to the ocean where the mermaid lives in order that he might enter into the love and happiness which she promises him.

The girl who gave Poko the book of stories invites him to come to see the travelling circus in which she and her brother perform. When Poko and his brother slip out that night and go to the nearby village where the circus is being performed, they are caught up in the wonder and joy of the crowd.

The next day when the father finds they have been away without his permission he confronts the older brother who for the first time stands up to his father and threatens to leave home. To show his determination he goes off for a few days to help with the circus in which the girl who gave Poko the book performs. When she asks him to become part of the circus he says he is not at present free to do so. This is a hard decision for him to make as it involves facing the fact that he will be the next victim in the feud with the neighbouring farm. We feel, however, that he makes it for Poko's sake. As it works out, the person who comes to claim his life is so afraid that he kills Poko instead.

The story ends with the older brother leaving the farm to search for the girl he loves. Before he goes in search of her he first makes his way to the ocean to honour his brother's dream.

CHAPTER 1

Two views of the Mass

In this chapter we will look at two views of the Mass. One of these views the Mass primarily as worship, or as something we do for God. The other views the Mass primarily as a revelation of love, or as something God does for us.

Keeping the dream alive

In the film *Behind the Sun* it was Poko's capacity to dream that kept him alive and happy in the joyless environment he lived in. This capacity to live, even for short periods, within an environment where love prevailed helped Poko to counteract the effect of living in a world dominated by hate. By constantly retelling the story about his love for the mermaid and her love for him he was able not just to maintain this world of his dream but also to expand it.

A revolutionary discovery

When I was in my early thirties and finishing off my studies as a Jesuit I made a discovery which was for me revolutionary. It was that the Christian life is more a matter of being loved than of loving. Up to that time I had believed that doing the will of God, seen as what we were meant to do for God, was the primary objective of the Christian life. The change in this way of believing was triggered off for me at a course given by the Indian Jesuit, Tony de Mello, when he told us about something very significant that was said to him at a critical stage in his life. When his mentor noticed that Tony was very preoccupied with the work he was doing he said, 'Tony, the revolution will occur in your life when you realise that life is not so much a matter of what you do for God as what God seeks to do for you.'

Two crucial experiences

There were two experiences that prepared the way for this revolutionary one. One was a course I attended on the Mass while studying theology. At the beginning of this course the lecturer made much of the fact that the Mass is primarily an experience of Grace or of 'the gift of God' (Jn 4:10) and only secondarily was it worship. He thought that most people saw the Mass as primarily worship or as something they did for God. What he said urged me on to a place I was, unknown to myself, already on the way to. It clarified and defined something I welcomed enthusiastically.

The second experience was an article I read by Karl Rahner. This stated that the basis of all theology and spirituality is the desire of the three persons of the Trinity to reveal themselves to each person. Therefore, we are basically receivers of the gift of themselves which the three persons wish to give when they reveal themselves to us. We are primarily receivers of 'the gift of God', called initially and primarily to be contemplative, to be listeners. Only after we have listened are we called to respond. This is what Jesus stresses in the parable of the Sower in which we are asked to hear the Word of God and to make our own of it or in the words of the parable to 'hold fast to the Word with a noble and generous heart'. (Lk 8:15)

Seeing the big picture

With time I gradually realised that my revolutionary discovery was part of a more universal one. In other words, this change in the way I saw the Mass was part of a similar change that was taking place in our way of seeing the Word of God, the church, the Christian life and the culture within which we live. We could imagine this revolutionary change as taking place within five concentric circles of experience, with the mass as the innermost one:

- In the innermost circle we have the radical shift from seeing the Mass primarily as worship to seeing it primarily as

Grace. In this book we will be seeking a better balance between these two aspects of the Mass, between seeing it as a contemplative experience and an active response, between the Mass being something God does for us and something we do for God.

- The circle representing our experience of the Word of God surrounds the circle representing our experience of the Mass. Here there is also a radical change taking place as we move towards seeing the Word primarily as the story of the revelation of God's love. In the past we tended to see the Word mainly as a source of meaning and we tended to focus on the implications of this for the way we live. The way we choose to see the Word or the view of it we adopt is important as it has a profound influence on the way we see the Mass. So, if we adopt the view that the Word is the whole story of the revelation of God's love and that the Mass is the climax of this story, then the Mass becomes a remembering of the supreme moment in the revelation of God's love.

- In the circle surrounding the Word of God we have a radical change taking place in our view of the church. We see this in a movement away from identifying the church with its institutional element to emphasising more its intellectual and prayer elements. This movement focuses on the vision that gives the rules and ritual of the institutional element their meaning and importance. This revolutionary change in our concept of the church, where the institutional, intellectual and prayer elements are held in a healthy balance, has been explored in an article called, 'Faith Under Survey' by Liam Ryan that appeared in *The Furrow* in 1983.

- In the next circle is our changing view of ourselves as Christians. In the 50 years since I decided to become a priest I have seen a revolutionary change in our way of viewing the Christian life. The emphasis has shifted from doing God's will as doing things for God to being receptive to what God plans to do for us, to 'knowing the gift of God'. (Jn 4:10) The emphasis has shifted to answering the essential call of the Christian to repent and believe the good news. In this context the Mass becomes the supreme moment in the revelation of this good news.

- In the outermost circle we have a revolution that has occurred in the cultural setting in which we live. Ours is an excessively active culture, dominated by what we do and what we acquire, but there is also a minority culture that is on the rise. This is termed 'the rising culture' in F. Capra's book, *The Turning Point*. There he describes a movement away from a materialistic worldview and value system and towards one which emphasises how we relate. In this context the Mass is a space we are given to become aware of the extent and depth of the love of Jesus and how it draws everyone and everything into relationship with one another in drawing all to himself. (Jn 12:32) Mass becomes primarily a time for wonder, contemplation, appreciation, celebration and gratitude.

In this setting, which we looked at in the five circles above, two views of the Mass compete for our allegiance. One of these sees the Mass primarily as worship or as something we do for God, the other sees the Mass primarily as Grace or as something God does for us, God's self-disclosure as love for us. What this book seeks is a healthy balance between these two points of view.

The healthy balance that Jesus sought between the active and the contemplative side of us is expressed in the story of Martha and Mary. (Lk 10:38-42) Martha, who is concerned about many things, represents the predominantly active approach to life, whereas Mary, who sat at the feet of Jesus listening to him, represents the predominantly contemplative approach. In reflecting on this story over the centuries Christians were led to believe that life, while being a mixture of active and contemplative elements, needs to be predominantly contemplative. They were led to believe that as Christians we are primarily listeners to God's self-revelation. Only as a result of this listening do our hearts tell us how to respond. Our life is God's gift and our basic response is to receive it.

God our Father,
gifts without measure flow from your goodness
to bring us your peace.
Our life is your gift.
Guide our life's journey,
for only your love makes us whole.
Keep us strong in your love.
(Opening Prayer of Week XVIII)

Paul, in his letter to the Ephesians, warns us of the danger of our human tendency to earn our worth rather then to receive it as a gift:

For by grace you have been saved through faith, and this is not your own doing; it is the gift of God not the result of works. (Eph 2:7-9)

John also, in his first letter, challenges our tendency to overesti-mate the importance of what we do for God. Our love is ab-solutely dependent on God first loving us and on our accepting this love in faith:

In this is love, not that we loved God but that he loved us and sent his Son to be the atoning sacrifice for our sins. Beloved, since God loved us so much, we also ought to love one another. (1 Jn 4:10-11)

There are three parts of the Mass that make it primarily a con-templative experience, a time when we 'see visions and dream dreams' before we start projects. (Acts 2:17) The three parts are, the readings, the consecration and the communion. Each of the three is accompanied by ritual and prayer by means of which we respond to what we have listened to. The times when we re-spond are, the offertory, the Eucharistic Prayer and the prayers that accompany the communion of the Mass. Seen from this point of view, the Mass takes the form of a dialogue or convers-ation. In this dialogue God takes the initiative and we are pri-marily listeners.

Some suggestions for reflection and prayer

1. Read the following story and describe what it says to you about the theme of this chapter. Are there ways you lose the plot or the big picture so that you are left with a lot of 'loose ends'?

> *Is it just loose ends?*
> When the leader who had just been appointed was asked what policies he intended to follow he answered by taking a simple illustration. It was of the miniature tapestries his mother used to make. He explained how she used to weave a design with various colours of wool onto a piece of strong gauze. When she was finished there was a very colourful design woven onto one side of the gauze. On the other side, however, there was a mass of disorganised loose ends. The leader then said that his ambition was to find and hold on to the design and to see all the details of his job in the light of it.

2. Outline a few key moments in the way your understanding of the Mass has developed. You could do this by dividing your life into a few periods and saying one thing about what the Mass meant for you in each of these periods.

3. After quietening yourself, become conscious of Jesus' presence. Allow him to be with you as one who wants you to be more than to do, to be with him as a companion before he sends you out as a disciple. (Mk 3:14)

4. In the light of your experience of 1-3 above reflect prayerfully on any of the following: Mk 3:14, Lk 10:38-42, 1 Jn 4:9-10.

CHAPTER 2

Four aspects of the Christian vision

In chapter 1 we saw that the Mass is primarily a vision of Jesus'
love for us and in this chapter we look at four aspects of this
vision.

Keeping the vision alive

In the film, *Behind the Sun*, it is vitally important for Poko to
keep his dream alive and the vision of a happier life it gives
him. This dream is constantly being eroded by the circumstances in which he lives. So we see him sitting under a tree
at some distance from his home dreaming about the mermaid at the centre of his story, imagining himself living happily with her beside the ocean. As he tells himself this story
he elaborates on the original version of it, changing and
adding to it as his imagination inspires him to. In this way he
lives out his fantasy of his love for her and of their happiness
in being together. Living in this environment that is warm
and joyful helps him survive in one that is hostile and sad.
Amid the grim circumstances he has to cope with each day
he builds a place where his dream of love, intimacy and joy
sustain him.

Grace seen in terms of friendship

I have still got the notes I made during a course that I attended
in 1964. I have gradually discarded most of the other notes I
made when I was a student but I have held on to these. What ex-
cites me about them is the vision of Grace they seek to express,
the vision of what it means to be a Christian. It is a vision of the
friendship Jesus initiates when he reveals himself to us, when he
gives us a gift of himself in self-disclosure. It is not a theoretical

vision but one of Jesus going around making friends and drawing people into his own relationship with his Father. (Jn 14:8-9)

This concept of Grace as a friendship has had difficulty in
taking root in the minds and hearts of Christians. Jesus' call to
become his friend, by sharing in his own relationship with his
Father, has seemingly been too challenging. As a result, this understanding of the Christian life as friendship with Jesus has
gone underground for long periods. Relying heavily on the following verse of John's gospel, St Thomas Aquinas sought to resurrect this image of friendship as central to our understanding
of the Christian life:

> I do not call you servants any longer, because the servant
> does not know what the master is doing; but I have called
> you friends, because I have made known to you everything
> that I have heard from my Father. (Jn 15:15)

The three elements of friendship
There are the following three elements in St Thomas Aquinas'
understanding of friendship:

- The first of these is that we wish all that is best for our friend,
  we wish to share with our friend what we value most. For
  Jesus this is his relationship with his Father and with the Holy
  Spirit. He wants to share 'everything' about this relationship
  with us, its glory or the radiance of its love, its profound intimacy and its complete and constant joy. (Jn 15:9-15)

- The second element of friendship is mutual sharing so that
  we return our friend's love as well as receive it. Just as Jesus
  shares everything with us by making known his inmost self,
  so we seek to share everything with him, our 'whole heart,
  soul, mind and strength', by 'abiding in' his love. (Jn 15:9-10)

- The third element involves ongoing communication through
  which we accept Jesus' invitation to listen and respond to the
  Word of God. (Lk 8:15)

A vision that has endured

The person who opened up for me this vision of Grace as friendship saw the gospels as the story of Jesus going around making friends with people and leading them into his own relationship with his Father. From the beginning to the end of the gospels Jesus initiates and develops this friendship by making known his Father's love. (Jn 1:18-17:26) Thus, each gospel story reveals some aspect of this love and initiates a conversation in which we listen and respond to Jesus. We listen to what he reveals to us about his love and about our lovableness in his eyes. We respond to this by telling him how we feel about his love and by gradually making our own of it.

Four aspects of Grace

In the remainder of this chapter we will look at the following four aspects of Grace understood as friendship. These will act as a backdrop for an understanding of the Mass to be elaborated on in the rest of this book.

- The three persons of the Trinity want to make known their love for each of us,
- and if we abide in this love,
- it transforms all our relationships,
- drawing us into an extraordinary union in which we share their glory and their joy.

1. God's self-revelation as love

In Part 2 we will examine how Grace, understood as friendship, is a gift which the three persons of the Trinity give in revealing themselves to us. It is an extraordinary gift in that they give us 'everything' they have and are, in their complete self-revelation. (Jn 15:15) This is what John means when he speaks of the Father, Jesus and the Spirit wanting to make themselves known to us in exactly the same way that they know each other.

I know my own and my own know me, just as the Father knows me and I know the Father. (Jn 10:14-15) When the Spirit of truth comes, he will guide you into all the truth; ...

> All that the Father has is mine. For this reason I said that the
> Spirit will take what is mine and declare it to you. (Jn 16:12-15)

The three persons reveal their love more by what they do than
by what they say. For example, God's self-revelation in the Old
Testament centres on the Exodus just as this self-revelation in
the New Testament centres on the death and resurrection of
Jesus. (Jn 3:16)

2. Abiding in Jesus' love

In Part 3 we will reflect on how we 'abide in' the love which the
three persons of the Trinity make known in disclosing themselves completely to us.

> As the Father has loved me, so I have loved you; abide in my
> love. If you keep my commandments, you will abide in my
> love, just as I have kept my Father's commandments and
> abide in his love. (Jn 15:9-10)

At the heart of these 'commandments' that we need to keep if
we are to abide in Jesus' love is the Great Commandment. In it
we are invited to receive God's love and to return it with our
'whole mind and heart and soul and strength'. (Lk 10:27) This
means that we involve our whole person, senses, feelings, intu-
itions and convictions in receiving and returning the love of
God.

3. A love that transforms

In Part 4 we examine how 'abiding in' Jesus' love can transform
us. This transformation is rooted in the belief that we are loved
by Jesus as he is by his Father. (Jn 17:23) This belief in turn requires 'repentance' or a revolutionary change of mind and heart.
(Mk 1:14-15) What enables us to make this profound change is
the growing attractiveness of Jesus as he makes the full extent
and depth of his love known to us. (Jn 17:26) The revelation of
his love in all its beauty reaches its climax in his death and resurrection. When he is 'lifted up' on the cross and in glory, he
draws all to himself, (Jn 12:32) reintegrating all that has been disintegrated by sin. (Jn 11:52)

'And I, when I am lifted up from the earth, will draw all people to myself.' (Jn 12:32) ... He did not say this on his own, but being high priest that year he prophesied that Jesus was about to die for the nation, and not for the nation only, but to gather into one the dispersed children of God. (Jn 11:51-52)

4. A love that leads to union and joy

In Part 5 we reflect on the nature of the union or friendship Jesus draws us into in sharing with us his own relationship with his Father. We will see how this friendship is characterised by glory, intimacy and joy. (Jn 17) The glory is the radiance of the love the three persons share with each other and with us. As we come to know Jesus' glory, or the radiance of his love, its magnetic attractiveness draws us into a profound intimacy with him that is characterised by a 'complete' and constant joy.

The glory that you have given me I have given them, so that they may be one, as we are one, I in them and you in me, that they may become completely one. (Jn 17:22-23) I have said these things to you so that my joy may be in you, and that your joy may be complete. (Jn 15:11)

How the Mass expresses all this

The readings, the offertory, the consecration and the communion of the Mass keep us in touch with what is central to Grace. The readings tell the whole story of the revelation of God's love, while we focus on the climax of this story in the consecration. Through the offertory we express our willingness to abide in this love in spite of the difficult change of mind and heart this involves. This is the price of the wonderful transformation which the Mass promises to bring about in us. In the communion of the Mass and the prayers that surround it, we experience the glory of Jesus and the joy and intimacy that his glory or the spectacular nature of his love draws us into.

Suggestions for reflection and prayer

1. What aspect of friendship expressed in the following quotations do you identify with?

'Friendship is the gift of self in self-disclosure.' *(A Greeley)*

'Friendship is the marriage of the soul.' *(Voltaire)*

2. Describe one or two stages in the development of a friendship you have that you treasure. What distinguishes this relationship from others that mean a lot to you?

3. Enter a dialogue with the person you wrote about in 2 above. Begin by writing down what you say to him or her concerning how you see and feel about your friendship. Let your friend reply and then write down what she or he says. Continue the dialogue until you have both said all you want to say to each other.

4. In the light of what you have experienced about friendship in 1-3 above, reflect prayerfully on any of the following pieces of scripture: Jn 15:15, Jn 21:1-18, Lk 10:21-24.

PART 2

The love we remember at Mass

In Part 1 we focused on a view of the Mass as primarily a vision of Jesus' love which we want to renew. We then outlined four aspects of this vision that provide a framework for understanding the Mass. In Part 2 we will look more closely at the first of these aspects of love that is central to the Mass, the passionate love of Jesus, or his love of us 'to the end'. (Jn 13:1) To draw out the meaning of this passionate love we will compare it to our experience of being in love. We will see how the intensity of Jesus' love of us calls into play all the other loves we are familiar with from our personal experience and from the Word of God. The chapters dealing with these themes are as follows:

Chapter 3 examines the love which is central to the Mass.

Chapter 4 describes how this love is related to other loves that expand and deepen our experience of it.

Chapter 5 looks at how we can draw on our personal experience to make the love which is revealed in the Mass more tangible and attractive.

Chapter 6 reflects on the Word of God as the story of God's self-revelation and how it provides a context for understanding the love Jesus expresses for us at Mass.

Chapter 7 focuses on the method the Mass uses to remember Jesus' love.

Italian For Beginners

The story of the film *Italian for Beginners* centres on six people who come together each week for a class in Italian for beginners. They are all fragile people trying to deal with their own problems and those of others. The holding environment of each of them has become eroded with the result that they feel insecure and vulnerable.

Andreas is the local pastor who is struggling with his wife's suicide and how to make the word of God relevant to himself and to his parishioners in the light of all that has happened to him. Olympia is a baker's assistant who is drawn to Andreas when she meets him at the Italian classes. She finds he gives her a sense of a self-esteem that has been lacking in her life.

Halvfinn is a bar manager in a hotel and is so full of anger that he is aggressive and spends a lot of his time arguing with the customers. He is helped to channel his energies along more constructive lines when he sets out to win the affection of Karen, the very attractive manager of the local beauty salon. Karen has her own problems as she struggles to run her business and to cope with the frequent demands of her mother who is an alcoholic, seemingly determined to drink herself to death.

Jorgen is the manager of the hotel where Halvfinn works but is too gentle to be a success in an aggressive business world. He is also too shy to take the steps he needs to if he is to win the heart of Giulia, the beautiful young Italian girl who works for him in the hotel. She in turn hopes that Jorgen will notice her and perhaps ask her out. She is a lighthearted person adding a welcome relief to the otherwise sober atmosphere that surrounds most of the other characters in the film.

These six people seek a holding environment, a person or persons with whom they will feel significant, cared for and secure. Gradually, this begins to emerge for them as they meet regularly for their classes in Italian to which they are drawn for very different reasons. However, it is on a holiday they all go on to Venice that Jorgen and Giulia reveal their feelings for each other, Halvfinn is transformed by Karen and Andreas and Olympia find in each other the love they have lacked up to this point.

As the film concludes, our hope for each of these six very human characters is that their relationships will continue to deepen and that they will be able to maintain the life and happiness they have begun to find in each other's company. We get a glimpse of the possibility of this happening at a meal with which the film ends. At it they joyfully gather together to share what is happening for them and to nourish themselves with the affection they have for each other.

CHAPTER 3

He loved them to the utmost extent

In this chapter we will look at the passionate love of Jesus, or his love of us 'to the utmost extent', that is central to the Mass.

Transformation

The story of the film, *Italian for Beginners* focuses on six people and the dramatic effect that falling in love has on each of their lives. As we look at them before and after this moment-ous event we notice how falling in love affects their whole person, how it changes the way they see and feel about them-selves and each other and revolutionises the circumstances in which they live. As we look at them before someone wins their heart we see very ordinary lives where nothing much is happening, where everything looks drab and unfocused. Then when they fall in love we see how colourful and focussed they become, how they are transformed.

The most dramatic of loves

An image that is used to capture the more dramatic effects of Grace, or the fact that the 'love of God has been poured into our hearts by the Holy Spirit', is that of being in love. When the the-ologian Bernard Lonergan wrote *Method in Theology* in the early seventies I was intrigued to find him describing Grace as 'the dynamic state of being in love with God'. More recently, when asked to write a short piece describing why I became a Jesuit I found myself using this same image of passionate love. It sur-prised me and even made me feel a little uneasy to speak about my life in these terms but they were the most apt I could think of. Over the years there have been a number of aspects of this being in love experience that have struck me as I watched its effect on my brothers and sisters and on my nieces and nephews.

When I was in my twenties and thirties I always thought of being in love as the reserve of married people. It was only in my forties, inspired by C. S. Lewis' *Four Loves*, that I began to realise something about being in love that was more implicit than explicit in what he wrote. This is that there are four aspects of the experience of this kind of love that can be as real for somebody like myself who did not marry as for those who do. The four are worth dwelling with as they have a lot to say about interpreting the Mass as an experience of the passionate love of Jesus for us.

Important features of being in love
The first thing we notice when we fall in love is that someone becomes the centre of our attention. Everything begins to circulate around this person. We notice too that our whole person – heart, soul and mind as well as our senses – becomes engaged by this person. We want to be with, to see, hear and touch the one who arouses such strong feeling in us. We become very perceptive at an intuitive level as we seek to know more and more about the one we have fallen for. At the deepest level of involvement, convictions develop about who the other person is and about his or her importance for us. With time we may become convinced that life would not be worth living without this person.

One of the more obvious features of falling in love is its intensity. We speak of people being swept off their feet, being bowled over and falling head over heels in love. As this experience of intensity develops it normally quietens down. It may even seem to have disappeared, especially in times when a relationship is under strain. This quietening is often a sign that the intensity is moving from an excessive reliance on the sensate and feeling levels of experience to a more balanced reliance on intimations about who the other person is and about what he or she means to us. In time we rely more and more on our convictions about who the other person is and about his or her importance for us.

What is most impressive about passionate love is its power to transform us. It has a revolutionary effect on our life in that it moves us out of ourselves to make the interests and feelings of another the centre of our concern. It can transform us increasingly from being self-centred to being other-centred.

No greater love

We will now use these four features of being in love to help us to understand the kind of love that Jesus gives us a vision of at Mass. It is a vision of what Jesus calls 'the greatest love', the climax of the revelation of love of which the whole Bible is the story. (Jn 15:13) This is the love we are asked to savour and as-similate at Mass when Jesus invites us to eat his body 'given up' for us and to drink his blood 'poured out for' us. When John comes to describe the love that inspired Jesus to 'give up' his life for us he says that Jesus loved us 'to the end'. This phrase 'to the end' can also be translated as 'to death' or 'to the utmost extent'.

Being God's beloved

In our effort to understand something as mysterious as the love Jesus expresses for us at Mass, we need to work with an image of it that might make its extraordinariness more tangible and en-gaging. To do this we will use our experience of being in love or of passionate love. The use of this image to illustrate God's or Jesus' love for us has a long history. It has its roots in the Bible where the fact that we are God's beloved is revealed to prophets, like Isaiah, Hosea and Jeremiah.

> You shall be a crown of beauty in the hand of the Lord ... You shall be called My Delight Is in Her, and your land Married; for the Lord delights in you, and your land shall be married. For as a young man marries a young woman, so shall your builder marry you, and as the bridegroom rejoices over the bride, so shall your God rejoice over you. (Is 62:2-5)

At his baptism Jesus understands himself to be 'the Beloved' of God, when he hears God saying, 'This is my Son, the Beloved, with whom I am well pleased.' (Mt 3:16-17) We too are 'the

Beloved in whom God delights' since we are in Christ. (Acts 9:4-5) Because of this identification with Jesus, one of the Sunday prefaces expresses the extraordinary belief that God sees and loves in us what he sees and loves in Jesus (Preface of Sundays VII). Inspired by this belief, Paul in his letter to the Christians in Rome addresses them as 'God's beloved in Rome'. (Rom 1:7)

This image of ourselves as God's beloved has been used by people as diverse in time and place as Origen and Teresa of Avila, John of the Cross and Bernard Lonergan. We have a very revealing use of this image in Patrick Leigh Fermor's book, *A Time to Keep Silence*. In it he describes his experience of visiting five famous European monasteries. In one of these, curious to find out what drew the monks to their unusual way of life, he says:

> I asked one of the monks how he would sum up, in a couple of words, his way of life. He paused a moment and said, 'Have you ever been in love?' I said, 'Yes.' A large Fernandel smile spread across his face, 'Good,' he said, 'It is an exact parallel.'

Judging from how central romantic love is to so many of the stories we come across in our novels and films, it would seem to be as central to our secular imagination today as it has been to our religious one. Robert Johnson, in his book, *The Psychology of Romantic Love*, holds that romantic love is the greatest source of energy in the Western psyche. He sees it as having taken over from religion as our main source of meaning and ecstasy.

Passionate love in the gospel story
As we read the gospels we see something happening to the disciples that is similar to what happens to us when we fall in love. We see how they experienced the four qualities of being in love that we outlined above. First of all, we see Jesus making himself known to his disciples and becoming so attractive that they 'leave everything' to be with him. In spite of the difficulties of doing this they continue to centre their lives on him even when

others decide not to walk with him any longer. When in response to many of his disciples leaving him Jesus asks those
who remain if they too want to leave him, Peter answers, 'Where
can we go if not with you?' (Jn 6:68) For Peter, life has become in-
conceivable without Jesus. John too captures the magnetic effect
Jesus has on people with the words, 'the whole world is running
after him'. (Jn 12:19) In his description of Jesus' passion and
death John portrays Jesus as the Lord and King of people's
hearts. (Jn 18:37)

From the time the disciples accept the invitation of Jesus,
'Come and see' (Jn 1:39) his attractiveness engages them more
and more. The injunction of the Great Commandment (Lk 10:25-
27) to get their whole person, 'heart, soul, mind and strength' involved in God's love is something they are gradually drawn into
as they learn to 'abide in' Jesus' love. (Jn 15:9-10)

When the disciples are drawn to get their whole person involved in meeting and coming to know Jesus, his attractiveness
becomes increasingly intense. We see just how intense this becomes in the extraordinary decision of the disciples to leave
everything in order to be with him. But it is in his death that the
intensity of his attractiveness reaches its climax. In being 'lifted
up' on the cross and in the glory of his resurrection, his attractiveness becomes so powerful that he draws everything and
everyone to himself. (Jn 12:32)

The intensity of Jesus' love has a transforming effect on his
disciples. A sign of this is their willingness to leave everything to
be with him, to centre their lives on Jesus rather than on themselves, to undergo the revolutionary change of mind and heart
that belief in Jesus calls for. (Mk 1:14-15) This change is revolutionary for nothing transforms the way we see ourselves as
much as our belief in the way Jesus sees us and nothing transforms the way we see others and all creation as the way we see
ourselves. Our experience of Jesus' love of us 'to the end' empowers us to love others as he has loved us. (Jn 15:12)

What brings this transformation about more than anything
else is remembering at Mass that we are loved passionately or

'to the utmost extent'. The way the Mass urges us to remember that we are loved to this degree is primarily through the consecration. In it we accept Jesus' invitation to 'eat' and 'drink' or to savour and make our own of the love his body and blood symbolise. The fact that his body is 'given up' for us and his blood is 'shed' for us highlights the intensity or the passionate nature of the love that we are invited to eat or assimilate. In the words, 'for you and for all' Jesus draws our attention to the fact that each of us is the object of this passionate love.

In the words of consecration Jesus also says that his blood, which he sheds out of love for us, is an expression of the permanence of his love. Whereas we find it hard to maintain a passionate love in the face of infidelity, Jesus' love knows no such limitation for he says his blood is an expression of his everlasting commitment to us in the New Covenant. This commitment is not terminated when we sin and break the Covenant, for his blood is shed 'so that sins may be forgiven'. This means that the intensity of his love when he is 'lifted up' before us at Mass engages our whole person, drawing us together and to him. The disintegrating effect of sin is undone when he draws us to himself through the extraordinary attractiveness of his love. (Jn 12:32)

Finally, Jesus wants us to do all this 'in memory of' him, to keep alive the ultimate drama of the events of his death, and of the extent, depth and intensity of his love of us 'to the end' that his death demonstrates. By remaining in touch with this extraordinary vision of his love we are challenged to accept our own lovableness and that of others in his eyes.

Suggestions for reflection and prayer

1. Being in love is one of the most important experiences in our lives. What expression of this love in the following two quotations do you identify with most?

> 'Romantic love is the single greatest energy system in the Western psyche. In our culture it has supplanted religion as the arena in which men and women seek meaning, transcendence, wholeness and ecstasy.'
> (*The Psychology of Romantic Love* by Robert Johnson.)

> Set me like a seal on your heart, like a seal on your arm.
> For love is strong as death, passion as relentless as Sheol.
> The flash of it is a flash of fire, a flame of Yahweh himself.
> Love no flood can quench, no torrents drown.
> Were a man to offer all his family wealth to buy love,
> contempt is all that he would gain.
> (*The Song of Songs 8:6-7*)

2. Describe what you remember most about an experience of being in love that you have had.

3. Read the poem below and then imagine yourself being with Jesus and let him ask you the question the poet was asked. After reflecting for a while write down a few possible answers you could give and then choose one that would express your deepest desire.

> And did you get what you wanted from life, even so?
> I did. And what did you want?
> To call myself beloved, to feel myself beloved on the earth.
> (Raymond Carver, *Late Fragment*)

4. In the light of 1-3 above reflect prayerfully on any of the following passages of scripture that appeal to you: Is 62:2-5, Ps 42:2-5, Song 2:10-14, Lk 12:49, Jn 13:1, Jn 12:19.

CHAPTER 4

The all-inclusive love we remember

In chapter 3 we looked at how passionate is the love Jesus expresses in the Mass. In this chapter we will look at how all-inclusive this passionate love is in that it incorporates many other aspects of Jesus' love, how 'long and broad, how high and deep' it is. (Eph 3:18-19)

An all-inclusive love

There is a common way the six characters in *Italian for Beginners* are affected by their experience of falling in love. We see how falling in love is for all of them an intensely personal and joyful experience while we know that the future will challenge what can remain an impermanent and superficial love to become more permanent and profound. If they accept this challenge we anticipate that their love will mature into a friendship in which there is a mutual sharing of what is deepest about themselves.

The miracle worker

Being close to the end of a family of ten I was in a good position to observe the dramatic effect of falling in love on my brothers and sisters. Its effect touched on the miraculous for it could change beyond recognition siblings who in their adolescent years tended to be touchy and self-centred at times. Then all of a sudden they underwent this dramatic change, becoming easy to be with, outgoing and full of the joys of life. They became so tolerant, affable and generous towards their little brother that I was sorry that someone had spirited them away and that they were not around as much as before.

We have seen how transforming being in love can be, how it

can influence all the ways we relate, all the ways we receive love and return it. In other words passionate love is such that it calls a lot of other loves into play. Some of these loves act like a foundation it builds on and others it needs if it is to mature. In other words, the potential for some of these loves, such as affection, has already been developed before we fall in love but what affection has taught us often remains a dormant wisdom until the experience of falling in love arouses it and makes it operative. The development of other forms of love, such as fidelity, is called for if the potential for friendship that being in love possesses is to be realised.

Like the facets of a diamond

In the late 80s I wrote a book called *Nine Faces of God*. These nine aspects of God's love emerged from my daily reading of the Bible over many years. They are very distinctive ways God loves us and are clearly portrayed in the Bible story. Since we are made in God's image, in the likeness of one who *is love*, we have the ability to know from the inside what these nine kinds of love are like and how to receive and return each of them. However, even though we can know these loves from our experience we may not have articulated what distinguishes them from each other nor how well each has developed in the way we relate.

These nine aspects of love are like nine facets of a diamond. Each facet reflects the light in its own distinct way or has its own unique splendour but it is the combination of all the diamond's facets that reveals how resplendent the diamond is. This image of the diamond highlights the many faceted radiance of God's love that the Mass seeks to make us more aware of. Though the passionate love of Jesus, which we examined in Chapter 3, is central to what we remember at Mass, there are a cluster of other well-defined loves surrounding it. Each of these, like the profound or personal nature of God's love, has its own peculiar beauty to add to the passionate love that is central to the Mass.

Is your God too small?

An effect of focusing on the Mass as primarily worship has been the neglect of the Mass as a vision of God's love in all its splendour. As a result of this neglect, our image of God tends to remain static, part of a body of truths we have given our assent to. We may never have withdrawn this assent but we may never have challenged ourselves to expand and deepen it either. For example, what do the opening words of the Apostles' Creed, 'I believe in God, the Father Almighty' mean for us?. Do they speak of a powerful, transcendent and remote God, or of one who is love in all its splendour, an all pervasive providence? To put this question in more practical terms we might ask ourselves, 'Do we believe that God is as sensitive, kind and provident as the most loving people we know? Is God as radiant in his and her loving as the most strikingly loving person we know?'

The basic call of Jesus to 'repent and believe the gospel' challenges us not just to accept the passionate nature of Jesus' love but to expand and deepen our belief in the many other forms it takes. We are called to believe in what Paul speaks of as 'the length and breadth and height and depth of the love of Christ'. This is a vision of love that overwhelms us with its variety and its depth, a vision of 'all the fullness of God'. (Eph 3:17-19)

The capacity to explore the variety of ways we are loved is given to us by the Holy Spirit whose love 'has been poured into our hearts'. (Rom 5:5) We are led by the same Spirit 'into all the truth' or into the many forms this love is given by Jesus in the gospel stories. We are thus led bit by bit into 'all the fullness of God' according as we are ready to grasp it. (Jn 16:13-15)

A sequence of loves

There are a number of well defined kinds of love that the Spirit leads us into. We find each of these loves and the sequence in which they emerge in the Word of God and in our personal experience. Looking at each of these different kinds of love will give us a concrete picture of the extent and depth of the love the Mass seeks to keep us in touch with.

At the centre of these different kinds of love we are being led into is what we have called *passionate love*. This love which John describes as love 'to the utmost extent' is for Jesus the greatest expression of love the world has ever known. (Jn 15:13) In the remainder of this chapter we will examine some of the other loves that passionate love is founded on and finds fulfilment in. In other words, we will see how four of these loves lead up to or prepare for our experience of the passionate love of Jesus and then how another four help this passionate love find fulfilment in friendship.

Laying the foundation

Affection is a general term for the four loves that lay the foundation on which our lives are built. These four are the love that appreciates and accepts as well as the love that is personal and provident. As children, affection provides us with our first experience of a holding environment, of a place where we are appreciated and accepted. Being *appreciated* by our parents is an important part of our experience of affection. Each stage of our growth, from our first faltering steps to the first words we speak, is noticed and delighted in by them. As well as learning what it is like to be appreciated, we learn what it is like to be *accepted* when we misbehave and are disruptive or when we fall short of their expectations.

A *personal* love that we have already been initiated into in the home, where as infants we hold centre stage, often becomes more defined for us when we go to school. I remember the first friend I made when I went to a boarding school and was deprived of the affection of my parents, brothers and sisters. I was nobody in this new environment until I met Pewi. He was the first person who, as it were, called me by my name for he chose me and sought me out. We do not choose our family and so it is when at school we are singled out from the crowd and chosen by our companions that we become aware of the special flavour that personal love has.

When as adults we leave home in a permanent way we learn

to fend for ourselves. It is probably in these circumstances that we realise for the first time how much our parents have done for us and the value of the holding environment they have provided for us. In circumstances like these we become aware of the meaning of *provident love* and of its importance, of the meaning of the saying, 'It is care that makes and sustains us.'

... that passionate love builds on
When we fall in love we get a taste of what *passionate love* is like, of how its intensity calls into play all the ways of loving we have already learned. It engages our whole person in the pursuit of the beloved who becomes the centre of our world. In this way passionate love has the power to transform us. It takes us out of ourselves and teaches us how to make the changes which are necessary if we are to live happily with those we love. However, to maintain this transformation, passionate love needs to develop four other loves if it is to fulfill its promise. It needs to become permanent and profound so that it develops into the love called friendship that has at its core a joyful love.

Permanence is the primary need of passionate love if it is to mature. As C. S. Lewis remarks in his book *Four Loves*, passionate love tends to be the most impermanent of loves. Thus, it needs to develop its capacity to become a faithful, a constant or a *permanent love*. For love to become permanent it needs to be based on conviction rather than rely too much on physical presence and feelings of closeness. This means that for love to become permanent it needs to rely more and more on the glimpses we get of the goodness of others and on our capacity to convert these glimpses into convictions. It is these convictions that endure even when the other is physically absent or emotionally distant. Developing these convictions is very challenging for it involves noticing and articulating the glimpses we get of the other person. It also involves staying with these glimpses until they become part of what we believe to be true and worthwhile about the other person. This opens up the possibility of sharing with the other the good we find in him or her and all that this affirmation can do for our relationship.

As passionate love learns to rely more on our convictions about the one we love, it becomes more *profound* as well as more permanent. How profound this love becomes depends on the level at which we relate. Initially we tend to rely on the sensate and feeling levels at which we relate as we recount the events we share experiences of and how we feel about these. However, as the relationship develops we are drawn to share the insights we get into each other. What draws us to overcome the difficulties of doing this is the profound need we have throughout our lives for acceptance and affirmation. This requires that we learn to notice and share the insights we get into each other and the convictions we have come to about each others' goodness and beauty.

Out of our experience of a relationship that has become permanent and profound comes a *joyful love*. The nature of this joy or happiness is well expressed in Victor Hugo's saying that 'The supreme happiness in life comes from the conviction of being loved.' Though there is an obvious and important joy that we get from our senses and from the warm feelings that surround a good relationship, it is a joy that comes and goes. If we are to have a lasting joy we need to spend time with the insights we get into our own goodness and that of others. Even more so, we need to cultivate the convictions these insights put us in touch with if our joy is to be as constant and complete as Jesus would have it be. (Jn 15:11, 16:21-22)

... and finds fulfilment in friendship

When a relationship becomes profound, in the sense that we learn to notice, name and share what we find in each other and thus become affirming, we enter the realm of the love that Jesus calls *friendship*. (Jn 15:15) As Jesus sees it, this love centres on a gift he gives us not only of all he *has* but of *himself* in self-disclosure. The giving of this gift invites us to listen to what Jesus discloses of himself and then to respond to it. In this listening and responding, our friendship becomes a mutual sharing.

The closeness of our friendship depends on *what we share*, whether this be an activity we share an interest in, or something more personal and self-revealing. The closeness of our friendship

also depends on *how we share* this or on the level at which we
share it. We can share what is going on for us and how we feel
about this but we can also learn to share the glimpses it gives us
into ourselves and others. Further, we can share the convictions
we have come to over the years about what is true and worthwhile for us, our personal convictions not just about what is true
but what is good and beautiful. Finally, friendship depends on
the quality of the sharing. Friendship, like all relationships, is as
close or intimate as the communication going on within it and so
it depends on two people's ability to listen and respond to each
other, on their ability to be listened and responded to.

A sequence of loves in the Word
When Christians reflect on the gospels, in the light of the whole
Bible story, they tend to see their lives in terms of the passionate
love of God described there. People like Origen, St Bernard, St
John of the Cross, down to Bernard Lonergan in our own time,
see the Christian life in terms of being in love with God and each
of us being God's Beloved.

In the Old Testament, God's *passionate love* is portrayed for us
by the prophets, but especially by the prophets Hosea, Jeremiah,
Isaiah and Ezekiel. (Hos 2:16-22) However, it is in the Song of
Songs that this passionate love of God receives its most intense
and colourful expression. (Song 8:6-7) The foundation for this
vision of God is laid in the Exodus where the experience of the affection of God for us is captured by the word *loving-kindness*. (Ex
34:6-7) This affection has four sides to it. It appreciates and accepts,
it is personal and provident. It *appreciates* our 'splendour' as a
share in that of God (Ezek 16:14) and it *accepts* our limitations and
sinfulness no matter how great these may be. (Ezek 16:1-63, Ps 50)

In the early books of the Bible the object of God's love is the
people as a whole but in the prophets, God's love is revealed as
personal. Each of us becomes the object of God's love, the apple
of God's eye. In Jeremiah's words God's love is for 'the least no
less than for the greatest'. (Jer 31:20, 31-34) From the experience
of the 'wonderful works of God' during the Exodus the *provident
love* of God became clear and all pervasive. In other words, God

provides for all our needs on life's journey (Deut 1:29-33) so that there is nothing too great for this love to give us or too small for it to attend to. (Ps 139)

One of the most striking features of the passionate love of God in the Old Testament is its *permanence*. No matter how often we break the covenant God is faithful to us, for the covenant is an eternal one. (Ezek 16:59-60) The *profound* nature of this passionate love is also highlighted by prophets like Hosea and Jeremiah. (Hos 2:16-22, Jer 31:31-34) Guiding all this revelation of God's love is a plan for our peace or joy. God is a *joyful* lover who wants to share this joy with us. (Jer 29:11) Finally, the love called *friendship* is the ultimate object of God's self-revelation in Jesus. This friendship that initially Abraham and Moses were called to, is now open to all of us. (Ex 33:11, Jn 15:15)

Nine portraits of love in the gospels

In the life of Jesus we find the fullest expression in human terms of these nine loves we have looked at in the Old Testament. In these nine we are given a vision of Jesus' 'glory', the radiance, splendour or beauty of his love. (Jn 1:14) Central to this vision as the greatest sign of his love is Jesus' death and resurrection. (Jn 15:13) Leading up to this most *passionate* expression of Jesus' love we have the gradual emergence of it, for example in the story of Zacchaeus. (Lk 19:1-10) The key to Jesus' relationship with Zacchaeus is his *acceptance* of him. We see this acceptance in the way Jesus singles him out as the one he wants to eat with, even though Zacchaeus, as a chief collector of taxes, is an outcast. We see Jesus' *appreciation* of Zacchaeus when he says that his dignity, as a son of Abraham, is the same as anyone else's. The *personal* love of Jesus for Zacchaeus is portrayed for us in the way he makes him the centre of attention. He calls Zacchaeus in from the periphery of the crowd and places him at the centre and there speaks to him face to face. We see the *provident* love of Jesus in his statement that what he does for Zacchaeus is part of a plan 'to seek out and to save those who were lost'.

In the resurrection scenes we see how faithful or *permanent*

Jesus' love is. Nothing that his disciples did – their desertion, denial or betrayal of him – can sever his relationship with them or diminish his love. In fact their infidelity seems to make his fidelity to them all the stronger. (Jn 21:15-17) How *profound* Jesus' love is emerges in John's commentary on the meaning of the resurrection in chapters 14-17 of his gospel. There Jesus tells us that the love he asks us to abide in is as deep as his Father's love for him. (Jn 15:9) Jesus also makes it clear that all he reveals to us is aimed at sharing his *joyful* love with us, a joy that knows no bounds. (Jn 15:11) Finally, in opening up to us 'everything he has heard from his Father' Jesus initiates a love he calls *friendship.* (Jn 15:15)

How the Mass remembers these loves

The different kinds of love we have looked at in this chapter are expressed in the Mass as a whole but in three parts in particular, in *the readings, the Creed and the preface.* The readings express various aspects of the love of which the whole Bible is the story. The Creed focuses on the most significant events in this story and the preface focuses on the most significant events in the life of Jesus and the love these reveal.

The readings of the Mass fill in some part of the story of God's self-revelation of which the consecration is the climax. If the consecration is the expression of Jesus' love of us 'to the utmost extent', the readings reveal different aspects of what Jesus calls his greatest love. Each day's readings reveal a facet of the diamond that symbolises some aspect of the love of which the whole Bible is a revelation. Thus the readings fulfill our need to go back regularly to the details of the story if its climax is to retain its significance, its colour and freshness.

The Creed we say at Mass on Sundays and feast days is a very different expression of revelation than the readings. Its various parts were composed in times of controversy, to state clearly and exactly what we believe about the three persons of the Trinity. Even though its form of expression is not as attractive as the story form we find in the readings, it is important for us to keep coming back to the basic truths that reveal the most fundamental aspects of the love we believe in.

The Preface is another part of the Mass where we focus on some aspect of Jesus' love and what aspect we focus on is determined by the period of the liturgical year we are in. The language used in the preface is more imaginative than that of the Creed. For example, the preface of the Sacred Heart uses one of the most profound images of the Mass, as a fountain of life and joy that has its source in Jesus' love of us on the cross.

Lifted high on the cross,
Christ gave his life for us,
so much did he love us.
From his wounded side flowed blood and water,
the fountain of sacramental life in the Church.
To his open heart the Saviour invites all men,
to draw water in joy from the springs of salvation.
(Preface of the Sacred Heart)

Some suggestions for reflection and prayer

1. From the various kinds of love we looked at in this chapter select the one that appeals to you most. Reflect on one of the pieces of scripture attached to it and notice how Jesus' love is portrayed for us in it.

2. After deciding which of these loves appeals to you most, tell the story of its emergence in your life. For example, recall the key events in which it took shape for you, the insights these events gave you into this kind of love and the feelings it arouses in you.

3. Meet a friend and let him or her ask you about your experience of being loved in the way you focused on above. Write down a few things that you and your friend say in the conversation that develops out of this.

4. Reflect prayerfully on the love you focused on in 2 and 3 above in the light of one of the pieces of scripture given to illustrate it in the body of this chapter.

CHAPTER 5

The hidden wisdom of experience

In this chapter we look at how we can draw on our personal experience to make the various kinds of love we looked at in chapters 3 and 4 more tangible and attractive.

The dignity of difference

Although the six main characters in the film, *Italian for Beginners*, all fall in love, it is a distinctive experience for each of them. This is because what happens to each is part of a unique story of how each of the six has been led to realise his or her dream of a loving relationship. No two experience what happens or how they feel about this in the same way. No two are given the same glimpses of what it is like to be loved or reach the same convictions about the meaning of their experience. Therefore, the love that they become aware of and learn to believe in is part of a unique stream of inner wisdom that runs through each of their lives. This creates an air of mystery about how each sees his or her experience and how they react to this. This unpredictability of each of the six adds colour and humour, realism and interest to the relationships the film focuses on.

The wisdom of experience

When I was in my thirties and early forties I spent 12 years in Africa. After I came home it was some time before I realised how deeply I had been affected by my years there. One of the most lasting effects of these twelve years was what they taught me about the value of our personal experience. Where this struck me most forcibly was in my work as a teacher with a special interest in Religious Education. When I began to teach this it was called Religious Knowledge and the method used to teach it focused on imparting as much knowledge of Christian doctrine as possible. There was little concern for the pupils' own experience and for their spiritual needs in the light of their own culture.

Education through experience

After an initial three years in Africa I came home for four years to complete my studies. I became interested in the writings of Ronald Goldman, particularly in the research he did into the attitudes of young people to religion. He discovered that they lived in two quite separate worlds and that their spiritual or Sunday world was quite small compared to their more material or weekday one. This separation was damaging for both their worlds for it meant that the spiritual or Sunday world became unreal and irrelevant and that the more material weekday world lost much of its meaning.

The solution Goldman devised for overcoming the damaging effects of this divorce between our two worlds consisted in getting people to become aware of the richness of their own experience, of their accumulated wisdom. Then, if the Word of God was addressed to the wisdom embedded in their experience, it would make the spiritual world of the Word more real and relevant, and their everyday experience more meaningful and engaging.

What is most telling about Goldman's method of delving into our experience is that it works. It takes a lot of time and effort to arouse our experience but when we do devise ways of doing this, the spiritual dimension of our lives becomes much more real and involving. All of us have an immensely valuable resource in our personal experience and it can become our chief means of entering and exploring the world God wants to reveal to us in the Mass.

How the wisdom of our experience becomes dormant

However, if we are to make use of the very valuable resource we have in our personal experience we must face the fact that it is a largely dormant resource. What makes the world of our personal experience so worthwhile arousing and remaining in touch with is that it is central to our inner world of relationships. For Jesus it is in the love we receive and return within these relationships that we find life. (Lk 10:25-28)

We will now look at the wisdom which is available to us from three areas of our personal experience that the Great Commandment guides us into.

1. Receiving and giving love

The basic reality that underlies all our experience as Christians is that we are loved beyond all measure or 'to the utmost extent'. (Jn 13:1) Each of us develops distinctive ways of receiving and returning this love. For example, one situation we find ourselves in may call for the love of affection, while another may call for a love that is loyal. Even though we experience these different kinds of love in their fullest and purest form in our relationship with God, we get to know them in more tangible ways from our experience of people. These are the people who make love real for us by opening up areas of our hearts to which God can then speak in a way that is concrete and engaging.

2. The four levels at which we relate

The Great Commandment, as well as urging us to receive love and to return it, invites us to do so 'with our whole heart, our whole soul, our whole mind and our whole strength'. These four – heart, soul, mind and strength – represent the four levels at which we relate or the four levels at which we experience love and respond to it. We will look briefly at each of these four ways Jesus invites us to 'abide in' his love or to immerse our whole person in it. (Jn 15:9-10)

... with all our senses

We initially take in love and return it with our 'whole strength', interpreted here as our five senses. It is in significant events, and in what we pick up about these events from our five senses, that we become involved in relationships. So, we begin to get involved with the love of which the Mass gives us a vision by listening to the sensate details of some aspect of this love in the readings of the Mass.

... with all our heart

Abiding in Jesus' love involves our 'whole heart', or the world of feelings that are aroused by the significant events of our own story, or by the events we recall in the readings at Mass. The importance of this world of feeling can be gauged from the fact that our feelings are at the core of love just as love is at the core of life. But feelings need to be cultivated for it takes a disciplined effort to create and maintain an environment in which feelings, such as wonder, appreciation, gratitude, celebration and hope, play a role that is commensurate with their importance. Negative feelings too, such as anger, guilt, sadness, fear and anxiety, need to be related to rather than repressed. Otherwise they can dominate our experience in an unhealthy way.

... with all our soul

To abide in Jesus' love means getting our 'whole soul' involved in taking it in. Here the term 'soul' is taken to mean the intuitive side of ourselves that can notice and name the glimpses of love we are given. These glimpses are inspired by the Holy Spirit who enlightens us and thus leads us bit by bit into 'all the truth', (Jn 16:13) This enlightenment 'is not an idea but the way someone looks at us'. (Henri de Lubac) For example, enlightenment may take the form of the glimpses we are regularly given of ourselves by those who accept and affirm us. If we understand enlightenment in this way, it means that we get a lot of it even in any one day. It also means that if the main element in Christian wisdom is this experience of being accepted and affirmed, then there is a stream of wisdom in each person's life. This stream of our accumulated wisdom grows wider and deeper as it flows from one end of our life to the other.

... and with all our mind

The most harmful area of our experience to neglect is that of being loved with what the Great Commandment calls our 'mind'. We tend to see the mind as our capacity to think but here we take it to mean our capacity to convert glimpses of being loved into convictions. The convictions we are dealing with here are distinct from the merely intellectual type in that they grow out of and are constantly fed by the sensate, feeling and intuitive levels of our experience. Thus, we each have within us a large body of convictions about our being loved and our being loving. These convictions are more a felt, interior knowledge than an intellectual, exterior knowledge and they form the vision and the value system that ultimately shapes our lives.

3. ... within four basic relationships

A third element of our personal experience the Great Commandment guides us into is that of the four relationships within which we receive and return love. These relationship with ourselves, with significant people, with other people and with all things are mutually dependent. For example, our relationship with ourselves is dependent on our relationships with the significant people in our life, especially with the three persons of the Trinity. Similarly, our relationships with others and with all things depend on our relationship with ourselves. This interdependence is reflected in Jesus' commandment that we love others – and all creation – as he has loved us. (Jn 15:12)

Love others as I have loved you

The first relationship of which we have a lot of experience, and the wisdom this offers, is that with what we might call 'significant people'. These are the people who are significant for us and for whom we are significant. While these people love us in a human and thus in a limited way, they give us an invaluable impression of what the love of the Father, of Jesus and of the Spirit is like. They have the capacity to make the love of the Trinity more real, colourful and engaging.

The second relationship the Great Commandment invites us to get engaged in is the one we establish with ourselves. This relationship and the wisdom it offers is experienced when we recall the significant events of our story and the feelings, insights and convictions that these events can put us in touch with. There are two sides of ourselves we need to become aware of. There is the limited and sinful side of ourselves that when accepted can lead to poverty of spirit (Mt 5:3), and the gifted and graced side of ourselves that when appreciated can lead to humility. (Mt 11:29) The balance between these two that we need to attain is expressed in the following prayer in which we ask that our limitations and weaknesses may not obscure our vision of God's glory or get in the way of the feeling of peace this vision inspires.

> Almighty Father,
> the love you offer
> always exceeds the furthest expression of our human longing,
> for you are greater than the human heart.
>
> Direct each thought, each effort of our life,
> so that the limits of our faults and weaknesses
> may not obscure the vision of your glory
> or keep us from the peace you have promised.
> *(Opening prayer of Week III)*

The third relationship which the Great Commandment invites us to get involved in is that with people who are outside the circle of those who, like our family and friends, have influenced our lives in a profound and enduring way. Though they are not 'significant people' in the strict sense, they have influenced our lives. They can range from those we have worked with, to people we have read about and whose lives have moved us, or they may be people who undergo some tragedy and to whom our heart goes out. Over our lifetime, there is a build-up of experience of how these people have been generative in our lives and we in theirs. If we notice and appreciate the ways these people have related with us and we with them, a body of wisdom emerges. It is a wisdom generated by our experience of the love of people who touch our lives from time to time and thus give us a valuable impression of who God is. They can make the artistry with which Jesus relates, or 'the gracious words that came from his lips' (Lk 4:22), very tangible and real.

'Tell the good news to all creation'

The fourth relationship, that with things, is probably the area of our experience we are most unaware of. The role we allow things to play in our lives depends on how we view and value them. For example, if we adopt the view that things are merely functional, to be used irrespective of the role God has given them, then we will most likely not respect or care for our environment and we may even abuse it. On the other hand, if we see everything in the world around us as wondrous, as part of a web of relationships that forms our holding environment, then we will respect all the things that form part of this environment.

For Jesus, everything in creation is part of the good news as it is a revelation of God's love and providence. Is this what Jesus means when he sends us to bring the good news to 'all creation'? (Mk 16:15) In the light of this mission which we are given, everything in creation is to be respected (Lk 12:22-30) as part of what is symbolised by Jacob's ladder, part of its downward movement in that everything is a revelation of God's love and providence and part of its upward movement in that everything leads us back to God. Seen in this way, every bit of creation can cause us to exclaim with Jacob, 'God was in this place all this time and I never realised it. Surely, this is the house of God, the gate of heaven.' (Gen 28:10-17)

> Thee, God, I come from, to thee go,
> All day long I like fountain flow.
> From thy hand out, swayed about
> Mote-like in thy mighty glow.
> *(G. M. Hopkins)*

Marrying our personal experience to the Mass

We have been looking at the stream of wisdom that runs through each person's life, a wealth of wisdom derived from our experience of relationships and from the love received and given within these. We have also seen that this wisdom is largely dormant but that if it is aroused it has an important role to play in making the Mass more real and relevant, more tangible and engaging. The Mass in its turn provides a context, a holding environment, which gives everything in our personal experience meaning, importance and purpose.

We see how Jesus, with powerful effect, seeks to marry our personal experience and the Mass when he meets two of his disciples on the road to Emmaus. When he first meets them they are sad and verging on despair. Jesus draws them out and after he has listened to them talk about their experiences he helps them to interpret what has happened in the light of the Word of God and of 'the breaking of bread'. As a result of this integration of their two worlds, what had been a source of despair and sadness now becomes a source of hope and joy. (Lk 24:13-35)

Some suggestions for reflection and prayer
1. Imagine your unique wisdom as a stream that runs from one end of your life to the other. What does the following saying or story say to you about the value of your own experience and the wisdom you get from it?

> Let us hang upon the lips of the faithful for the Spirit of God is on every one of them. *Paulinus of Nola*

In Search of the Priceless Jewel
A man came across a cave on his journey and, being curious, he entered it. There he discovered what was to be the inspiration of his life in the form of a priceless jewel. However, all he could do was gaze at it for it was in the keeping of a ferocious beast. As he gazed at it his whole being was engaged and when eventually he left he felt that all else in life from then on would be insignificant by comparison.

But he got on with life, married and reared a family and then when his life's work was done he said, 'Before I die, I must again glimpse the jewel that has been the inspiration of my life.' So he set out and made his way back to the cave where he again found the jewel. But now the monster guarding it had grown so small that he was able to take the jewel away with him.

2. Take one of the most significant events of your life and say briefly what happened. With a word or phrase describe how you feel as you recall this event. What is significant about this event that causes you to remember it? Does remembering the event put you in touch with something you value highly?

3. Enter your inner room where you find all the most important events of your life recorded in the pictures around the walls. Dwell with one of these pictures. As you look at it, Jesus joins you and comments in a very affirming way on your role in this event. Dwell with what he says to you and see what you want to say in reply.

4. Reflect on your experience so far in this exercise in the light of one or more of the following pieces of scripture: Deut 1:29-33, Ps 139, Lk 12:22-34

CHAPTER 6

The role of the Word of God in the Mass

In this chapter we will reflect on the Word of God as the story of God's self-revelation and how as such it provides a context for understanding the Mass which is the climax of this story.

The big picture

All the characters in *Italian for Beginners* are put in touch with a broader or more universal experience than their personal one and they use this to understand what is happening in their personal experience. For example, they all belong to a culture in which romantic love is a major element in the stories people come across in the films they go to and in the novels they read. It is in this context that the six people in *Italian for Beginners* automatically interpret what is happening to them. During the holiday they all go off together on to Venice and during the meal with which the film ends there is a recognition and a celebration of this common or universal love they are all caught up in.

I spent nine years studying philosophy and theology. These two fields of knowledge were meant to provide a context for understanding what has been revealed to us in the Word of God. Though I got enough from those years to have made them worthwhile, I have always been disappointed when I think of what might have been possible if these subjects had been taught in a more enlightened and imaginative way. There were exceptions to this general deficiency but these only served to highlight what was lacking in most of the courses. So much time was spent with barren intellectual arguments and in wandering around in abstractions that had little appeal for our minds and less for our hearts, our souls or our senses.

Two roads inward

It was only later that I became aware of another approach, one that finds symbols to be as important as ideas. This is an approach that people use when they want to deal with the deeper things of life, with their vision and values. In an effort to understand their experience they often tell stories in preference to thinking things through intellectually. In the age of science, economics and the consumer culture it is believed that telling stories does not get to what is essential. We have been taught to believe that thinking logically about the facts which we have ascertained is the best way to understand our world.

For me there is something arid or colourless about this approach to experience. From the time I learned to read I have been fascinated by stories for I could immediately resonate with the world they depicted. As a result, I have spent a lot of my leisure time over the years reading novels, listening to stories on the radio and going to films. Even though we had to work hard on the farm where I grew up there were always plenty of books around and time to read them if we wanted to make it. When the family finances allowed, my father gave us one day off each week. I nearly always went to town for the day and would often go to two films and spend time in second-hand bookshops searching for novels that would keep me going for the rest of the week. As I write this I am aware that my favourite way of spending my day off is still to go to a film and to have a root in some second-hand bookshop for novels I might read or share with others.

The Word as story

The fact that the Bible is the story of God's self-revelation as love has always been its great appeal for me. I remember well the event that moved me on from seeing the Word of God as a source of meaning and messages to seeing it as a series of stories, each of which revealed in an imaginative way some aspect of God's love. It happened at a series of lectures I attended as a student on how the gospels came to be written. The lectures were

given by David Stanley, a Canadian Scripture scholar. He envis-
aged the apostles being questioned about who Jesus was by
people who had never met him. To answer these questions, disciples like John and Luke collected a series of stories about the
Jesus they had come to know and wrote them down. In effect,
when we read these stories today, the evangelists say to us,
'Listen to these stories, and under the guidance of the Spirit, we
think you will come to know Jesus in the way we did.'

Mass as the climax of the story

The Mass is the climax of the story of God's self-revelation in the
Word. So, just as the Word provides a context within which we
can see the true meaning of the Mass, so both the Word and the
Mass provide a context within which we can better understand
our personal experience. This relationship of the Word, the Mass
and our personal experience can be pictured as three parts of a
bicycle – the wheel, the hub and the axle. The wheel symbolises
the Word, the hub symbolises the death and resurrection of
Jesus which the Mass re-enacts and the axle on which the wheel
turns symbolises our personal experience around which everything revolves.

Thus the Word and the Mass provide a setting within which
we can understand and evaluate all that happens to us, a context
in which we can discern what is true and what is worthwhile in
our daily experience. For example, from the narrower perspective
of our own experience many things may make us fearful, whereas
when they are viewed from the much broader perspective of the
Word and the Mass, these fears may appear groundless.

However, the secular world in which we live has lost this
broader vision and the perspective it gives. As a result it experiences a loss of hope and a sadness like that of the two disciples
Jesus joined on the road to Emmaus. They were in despair, fearful and sad because Jesus and all that he meant to them had disappeared. When Jesus, through the Word and the 'breaking of
bread', helped them find the real meaning of what had happened and restored their belief in his loving presence, they re-

turned to Jerusalem full of joy and enthusiasm. In the words of Luke, they say to each other, 'Were not our hearts burning within us while he was talking to us on the road, while he was opening the scriptures to us? That same hour they got up and returned to Jerusalem.' (Lk 24:32-33)

Three ways of viewing the Word

There are three ways of viewing the Word and the role it plays. So, we may look for the *meaning* of a passage of scripture or for its *message* or we may focus on the *glimpse of love* it offers us. For example, when we read the parable of the Good Samaritan the meaning may be the practical nature of Christian love, the message may be how practical our love ought to be and the glimpse of love it offers may be the rounds Jesus is willing to go to in his concern for each of us. The first view focuses on what is true, the second on a morally good way of acting and the third focuses on the graciousness or beauty of Jesus.

These ways of viewing the Word lead to two ways of approaching it. We can approach a gospel story seeking to understand its meaning and the implications of this for the way we live, or we can approach the story seeking to know the aspect of Jesus' love it reveals. These two approaches differ dramatically in their effects. With the first we often end up finding ourselves deficient in the way we live out the gospels and this can sap our energy, whereas with the second we are enlivened by the affirmation it leads to. Even though we may have been schooled to adopt the more corrective approach, the basic call of Jesus to 'believe the good news' favours the more affirming one.

If Jesus affirms us in each gospel story, it has a profound effect on the image of him and of ourselves we live with. We see the truth of this if we examine the way we form an image of ourselves and of others. From what people say and do we weigh them up and form an image of them, but also of ourselves as seen in their eyes. We refine this image in successive meetings with them and even though we may not articulate it, a clearly defined image emerges of the people we meet and of who we are for them. Even though we automatically adopt this intuitive approach to our daily experience we may have difficulty approaching the gospels in this way. We may be so busy searching for the meaning and implications of the gospel stories that we may not notice the profound glimpses of Jesus they offer us. For this reason Jesus regularly asks each of us the question that is at the heart of the gospels, 'And you, who do you say that I am?' (Lk 9:20)

Who do you say that I am?
Even though we have a natural facility to form images of people and ourselves from what they say and do, we are unconscious of most of these images. This is because we do not take the trouble to notice and articulate them. If we do take the trouble to notice and articulate the glimpses of Jesus we get as we read the gospel stories, they can put us in touch with and confirm a vision of him and of ourselves that is already established or that we believe in. The glimpses of Jesus we get as we meet him in the gospels may also invite us to broaden and deepen our image of him. We can do this if we are willing to stay with these glimpses until they become convictions about the way he loves and relates with us. Any conviction about Jesus and ourselves we are led to in this way involves what Jesus calls 'repentance'. (Mk 1:14-15) This is a change of mind and heart, a letting go of convictions that are at variance with what we are led by Jesus to believe in.

The call to repent
There are three things involved in this call of Jesus to repent. There is a 'change of mind' in the gradual acceptance of his vision and there is also a 'change of heart' involved in our gradual acceptance of Jesus' value system or of what he feels deeply about. Thirdly, this change of mind and heart calls for a change of lifestyle if this is to be consistent with our vision and values.

We have a strange tendency to focus our attention on this third element of repentance and to neglect the vision and the values that it is an expression of. It was when I began to concern myself with the formation of others as a teacher that I realised the truth of the saying, 'It's the vision that counts.' This primacy of vision rests on the belief that the way we see people or things determines how we feel about or value them and that our vision and values determine the way we behave.

The power of the Mass to transform us, or to change our minds and hearts so that we would believe the gospel, lies in the vision it puts before us. This is a vision of a love that is extraordinary in its clarity, depth and attractiveness. It is a vision of the greatest love the world has ever known and of ourselves as loved to this extent. (Jn 15:13) This vision which the Mass presents for us to gaze at and take in is, as we saw in chapter 4, the climax and the summation of all the other forms of love revealed in the Word of God.

Hearing and holding fast to the Word

There are two ways we can know Jesus' love as it is expressed for us at Mass. We can know it exteriorly as with our mind alone and interiorly as with the mind in conjunction with our senses, heart and soul. What is distinctive about this interior knowledge is that it involves our whole person. This is the way that Jesus in becoming a human being seeks to engage our whole person and not just our mind. Thus in each gospel story he says, 'Come and see!' or 'Come and get to know me,' (Jn 1:39) and not just the meaning of what I say.

The vision of Jesus that emerges as we come to know him in the Word of God is of necessity revealed to us bit by bit as this is the only way we learn anything. The bit we are ready to learn is indicated to us by the enlightenment and attraction of the Spirit 'leading us into all the truth'. The way we notice the 'truth' that we are ready to learn is through observing what strikes us as we listen to the readings at Mass.

> When the Spirit of truth comes, he will guide you into all the truth; ... he will take what is mine and declare it to you. All that the Father has is mine. For this reason I said that he will take what is mine and declare it to you. (Jn 16:13-15)

In the readings at Mass the Word of God provides us with an opportunity to listen to God's self revelation and to respond to this. In the first reading taken from the Old Testament or from the letters of the New Testament we are invited to listen. In the Responsorial Psalm, as the name indicates, we respond to what we have listened to in the first reading. In the reading from the gospel we listen to a description of events that surround the central one we wish to remember at Mass.

Suggestions for reflection and prayer
1. What does the following story say to you about the Word of God?

Light in our darkness
In AD 627 the monk Paulinus visited King Edwin in northern England to persuade him to accept Christianity. Before making a decision the king thought to consult his advisers. After they had discussed the matter at length, one adviser stood up and said, 'Your majesty, when you sit at table with your lords and vassals, in the winter, when the fire burns warm and bright on the hearth and the storm is howling outside, bringing the snow and the rain, it happens of a sudden that a little bird flies into the hall. The bird flies in through one door and flies out through the other. For the few moments that it is inside the hall, the bird does not feel the cold, but as soon as it leaves your sight, it returns to the dark of winter. It seems to me that the life of man is much the same. We do not know what went before and we do not know what follows. If the new doctrine can speak to us of these things, it is well for us to follow it.'

2. Tell the story of the role the Word of God has played in your life by describing briefly what it came to mean to you at a few key times in your life.

3. Imagine a world without the Word of God. List some of the ways you would miss it and then describe what you would miss most if it did not exist. Be with each of the three persons of the

Trinity in turn and say to each what their Word means to you, their desire to reveal themselves completely to you through their Word.

4. Reflect prayerfully on any of the following pieces of scripture in the light of your experience of 1-3 above: Lk 8:11-15, 1 Jn 1:1-4, Jn 16:13-15

CHAPTER 7

The ceremony of remembering

So far in Part 2 we have looked at the love we remember at Mass and how it is revealed to us through our personal experience seen in the light of the Word. In this chapter we will consider how the Mass provides us with a way of remembering and absorbing the love of which it is a revelation.

Nourishing ourselves on the love we remember
As *Italian for Beginners* comes to a close we may ask ourselves the question, 'Will these six people we have been with during the film be able not only to keep alive their love for each other but to expand and deepen it as well?' A major part of how they will do this is symbolised by the meal with which the film ends. During this they tell their story or share what is going on for them. They listen and respond to each other and are listened and responded to. As they become aware of their care for each other they enjoy what is the real nourishment of the meal they share.

In 1978 I returned home to Ireland after more than a decade in Zambia. I was curious to know whether the method of teaching Religious Education I had used there would work as well with adults as it had with the young people I taught in Africa. The method was one I discovered in the writings of Ronald Goldman and through these I learned the value of our personal experience in its own right, but also as a rich resource for exploring the Bible.

Then in the early 80s I was introduced to the writings of Ira Progoff. In his books, *At a Journal Workshop* and *Process Meditation*, he explained the background to a series of exercises he had developed. The aim of these exercises was to explore the extent and the depth of the wisdom each of us accumulates over a lifetime from our daily experience. I did two workshops on how to do these exercises and studied the background to these in his writings.

From working with Goldman and Progoff I realised the truth of their conviction that each of us has a profound wisdom available to us in our story. From Goldman I learned the vital role personal experience plays in making the wisdom of the Bible real and tangible as well as engaging. Progoff, on the other hand, taught me how to explore the extent and depth of my personal experience. He gave me a way of drawing on a rich vein of experience in what he calls *our underground stream of inner wisdom*. In providing a way of noticing, exploring and owning our personal experience, Progoff has opened up an enlightening model with which to understand what happens at Mass.

Progoff's method

There is an interesting parallel between the way we remember Jesus' love at Mass and the way Progoff explores the extent and depth of our experience. He calls the extent of our story *the horizontal dimension* of it and its depth *the perpendicular dimension*. The horizontal dimension of our story means that it stretches from one end of life to the other. The perpendicular dimension means that certain events in our story have a special significance which we are invited to explore.

To draw on the richness of the horizontal dimension of our story, Progoff recommends that we divide it into periods which he calls 'stepping stones'. Within each period he suggests that we note the main events, believing that remembering one event will trigger off the memory of others. Some of these periods, such as the present one, may be more significant than others so he advises us to develop these more fully.

In inviting us to explore the perpendicular or depth dimension of our story Progoff believes that there are important events in it that have influenced the meaning and direction of our lives.

Through getting in touch with this depth dimension of our story we discover a wisdom life has taught us. Unfortunately, this wisdom is largely dormant or is part of a stream of experience that flows well below the surface of our life. To avail of this wisdom we need to dig a well to draw on it. This involves working with the four levels at which we experience this wisdom which are the sensate, the feeling, the intuitive and the convictional levels at which we relate. Each of these four makes a distinctive contribution to our inner wisdom.

So, for example, if we wish to explore the relationship we have with our body, Progoff recommends that we tell the story of this relationship, then that we make a focusing statement of where we now are at present in our relationship with our body. He feels that we will then be ready to begin a dialogue with our body. If we allow our body to talk to us and then respond honestly to what we hear it saying to us, we will discover that the body has its own wisdom. We will find our relationship with our body enriching as we become more intimate with it, respect its wonder and realise what a good companion it is.

An enlightening parallel

There is an enlightening parallel between how Jesus asks us to remember him and his love at Mass and how Progoff invites us to keep in touch with the extent and the depth of our experience. The Mass has two ways of remembering. The first of these we will call, *telling the story* and the second, *breaking the bread*. We first of all tell the story of some aspect of Jesus' love of us and then we 'eat' and 'drink' this, or taste and digest it as we do with food. In the readings of the Mass we focus on the horizontal dimension, or the extent of Jesus' self-revelation, by remembering some part of the story of this. We then shift our attention to the perpendicular or depth dimension of the story when we 'eat' and 'drink', or savour and assimilate, some aspect of the love revealed in the story.

Telling the story

In the readings at Mass some aspect of the love which we remember in the consecration is highlighted. Which aspect is determined by each person's need, by the unique experience that each of us brings to Mass. There is always some aspect of the love, of which the Word is the story, that each person is ripe for or ready to listen to. We are each at our own unique place on our journey into the length and breadth and height and depth of the love of Christ. (Eph 3:17-19) The area of this love which we are ready to enter, explore and assimilate is made clear to us through the enlightenment and attraction of the Spirit. It is important to remember that this *enlightenment* is not an idea, a meaning or a message, but some aspect of Jesus' love revealed in the way Jesus treats, looks at or relates with us in the gospel story we focus on at each Mass. Since the enlightenment of the Spirit is a glimpse of Jesus' love, it has a built-in *attraction* for us as it reveals not just something we desire but something *we are a hunger for*.

In practice, the Spirit's enlightenment and attraction is experienced in a word, a phrase of the readings that strikes us, in an image or feeling we warm to. If this guidance of the Spirit is to be effective we need to notice and put words on the aspect of Jesus' love we are given a glimpse of. If we do not become aware of these glimpses, if we do not clarify what is being said to us and how we feel about this we become a part of the tragedy depicted in the parable of the Sower. The seed does not take root in us and yield a rich harvest if we do not 'hear the word of God and hold it fast in a noble and generous heart'. (Lk 8:11-15)

'The breaking of the bread'

One of the names of the Mass used by Luke in his gospel and in the Acts of the Apostles is 'the breaking of the bread'. He uses it, for example, at the end of his description of what happened to the two disciples Jesus joined on the road to Emmaus. There he speaks about how Jesus 'had been made known to them in the breaking of the bread'. But before this Jesus has put his sufferings and death in context by helping them to understand the meaning of these events in the light of the Word.

> They said to each other, 'Were not our hearts burning within us while he was talking to us on the road, while he was opening the scriptures to us?' ... Then they told what had happened on the road, and how he had been made known to them in the breaking of the bread. (Lk 24:32-35)

When Luke uses the phrase, 'the breaking of the bread' he highlights the fact that the Mass is a meal. At it Jesus invites us to eat the 'bread of life' or to eat his body and to drink his blood. (Jn 6:56) This eating and drinking involves making our own of the love symbolised by his body 'given up for' us and by his blood 'shed for' us. We 'eat', or make our own of this ultimate expression of Jesus' love, in the same way as we make our own of any experience that is important for us. We recall such an experience to listen to what it is saying to us and then we respond by saying how we feel about this. The purpose of this dialogue is to make our own of experiences that mean a lot to us and to believe what they are saying to us.

The dialogue the Word and the breaking of bread initiate
Jesus initiates a dialogue when he reveals himself to us in the readings but especially when he makes himself known to us in the breaking of the bread. For example, when we hear the story of Zacchaeus read at Mass, we are first of all invited to listen to the details of the story, to notice what is said and done. We are then invited to notice what glimpse of Jesus' love for Zacchaeus we get from the story. We are also invited to notice and express how we feel about this, whether we feel joy like that of Zacchaeus or resistance like that of the grumbling crowd. But the main question this story asks us is about our convictions or what we believe. Do we believe that what Jesus is saying to Zacchaeus about his love for him is said to us now? In each reading we hear at Mass, but especially in the consecration, Jesus initiates a dialogue when he asks us, 'Do you believe that I love you 'to the utmost extent' and that you are therefore utterly lovable?'

This dialogue that Jesus initiates when he 'breaks the bread' at Mass is the most effective way of savouring and assimilating the love it symbolises. There is no better way to 'eat' and 'drink' this love than by repeatedly listening and responding to it in prayer. This is the way that Jesus regularly recommends in the gospels for responding to his self-revelation in the Word. For example, in the parable of the Sower this is what Jesus says is necessary if the love which the Word reveals is to take root in us and to grow.

But as for that in the good soil, these are the ones who, when they hear the word, hold it fast in an honest and good heart, and bear fruit with patient endurance. (Lk 8:15)

The Mass as a dialogue
We will conclude this chapter by looking at how the Mass takes the form of a dialogue which Jesus initiates with each person when he reveals 'the depth of his love'.

He always loved those who were his own in the world. When the time came for him to be glorified by you, his heavenly Father, he showed the depth of his love.
(Eucharistic Prayer IV)

At the beginning of Mass we prepare to enter this dialogue by becoming aware, like Moses before the burning bush, of the awesomeness of the place we are in. Like Moses we are aware of our unworthiness and give expression to this in the Confiteor.

I confess to almighty God
and to you, my brothers and sisters,
that I have sinned through my own fault,
in my thoughts and in my words,
in what I have done,
and in what I have failed to do.

After thus disposing ourselves to 'speak to God face to face as with a friend' (Ex 33:11) we listen to some part of God's self-disclosure in the readings. We are reminded of this reality that it is God who speaks, by the words said at the end of the readings: 'This is the word of the Lord.'

The offering of our gifts at Mass is basically an offering of ourselves to God so that our minds and hearts may be transformed by what God reveals to us. It is a transformation that will entail the sacrifice of dying to the old self so that the new self which the Mass reveals to us may emerge.

Lord God, we ask you to receive us
and be pleased with the sacrifice we offer you
with humble and contrite hearts.
(The prayer of offering)

The consecration is the high point of God's self-revelation as it presents once again the death of Jesus out of love for us.

Take this, all of you, and eat it:
this is my body which will be given up for you.

The Eucharistic Prayer that is built around the consecration is our response to remembering again this supreme moment in history. It is therefore a prayer full of the most basic feelings of gratitude, praise and desire.

Father, all-powerful and ever-living God,
we do well always and everywhere to give you thanks
(Weekday Preface I)

The dialogue of the Mass is concluded in the communion and in the prayers that surround it. What we listen to here is the love Jesus expresses when he gives us his body to eat and his blood to drink. We rest with the intimacy and joy this leads to.

Our response to what the communion of the Mass reveals finds expression in the communion prayers. But this response is also shaped by what emerges in each person's heart in this most intimate moment in our life

Some suggestions for reflection and prayer

1. What aspect of the Mass does the following story and sayings highlight for you?

Counting your blessings

A very elderly married pair auctioned their house. As they sat for the last night in what had been their home, it seemed very bare. Just before they went to bed he took out a little tin box he had saved from the auction. In it were memories of their life together, of the ways they had been blessed, the joys they had shared, and even their times of darkness that had turned out to be blessings in disguise. As they took these out of the box and dwelt on each one in turn, they were no longer conscious of their stark surroundings. They re-lived the richness of their life together and they were grateful to God.

That night he died in his sleep. When he was laid out, she placed his box of memories with the rosary between his joined hands. It was with these she knew he prayed best. The evening of the funeral she opened her own store of memories and placed there all the words of appreciation of her husband she had heard at the funeral. In the years that remained to her, she was sustained on her solitary journey, by the grace-filled memory of their life together.

'Such good things can happen to people who learn to remember'. *(Emily Dickinson)*

'One day we will delight in the memory of these things'. *(Virgil)*

2. Outline the story of the Mass in your life by describing a few times when you grew in understanding of its meaning and of its importance for you. How do you see the role of the Mass in your life at present?

3. There are two sides of ourselves that we bring to Mass. One side tends to neglect the past as having little to say to us or if we do remember past events, it is only in a superficial way. The

other side of ourselves tends to take time to dwell with the important events of the past and to listen to what they have to say to us. Enter a dialogue between these two sides of yourself.

4. Reflect prayerfully on any of the following pieces of scripture in the light of your experience of 1-3 above: Deut 6:4-13, Wis 16:11, 1 Cor 11:23-26.

PART 3

Immersing ourselves in the love we remember

In Part 2 we looked at the love we remember at Mass and in Part 3 we will concentrate on how we listen and respond to this love so that we might learn to accept Jesus' invitation to 'abide in' it.

Chapter 8 examines how we listen to what Jesus reveals to us about his love at Mass.

Chapter 9 reflects on how listening to the love Jesus reveals to us at Mass arouses feelings that we need to find ways of expressing.

Chapter 10 looks at how by listening and responding to the love revealed to us at Mass we can change our mind and heart in order to believe in it.

Chapter 11 dwells with how suffering can bring about this same change of mind and heart.

Chapter 12 looks at how we learn to live consistently with what we believe by developing the art of loving.

Love and Loss

Sea of Love, Sea of Loss is a book written by John Quinn, an Irish writer and broadcaster. It is the story of how he met, fell in love with and married Olive and of the years they spent together before she died suddenly while swimming in the sea. Three things shape the story he tells. Two of these are clear and tangible but the third is mysterious and elusive. The two obvious ones are the extent and depth of the love he and Olive shared and then apparently lost when she died. The third is how he regained this love he thought he had lost in a new and mysterious way. Though this third element is intangible for us it is obviously very real for him. It emerges in the growing sense of her presence as he tells the story of their life together. Even though he knows that after her death he must travel most of the time alone and in the dark, his journey is still pervaded by the abiding presence of the love they shared, do share and will share.

And it was lovely then,
And you were lovely then,
And we were young and so in love,
And it was lovely then,
And will be so again,
And will be so again.
(John Quinn)

After an initial period when it was too painful to open his box of memories, he eventually got the courage to take them out one by one. Painful as it was to do this, he knew he had to resurrect and keep in touch with the love they shared. So gradually he begins to recall, to listen to and savour how they met and fell in love. He dwells with the letters they exchanged most days for the two years before they married. He recalls the glorious times of their life together as well as the difficulties which tested and refined their love.

As he tells his story he returns a number of times to the words of Virgil, 'One day it will delight us to remember these things'. He reveals his feelings of loss and almost unbearable loneliness and he describes the road he had to travel as a lonely and dark one in spite of the support of his family and friends. But he also reveals the deep gratitude and even the delight that he found in the memories of Olive and the extent and depth of the different feelings that each memory evokes for him. His expression of these feelings plays a huge part in revealing what the love they received from and gave to each other meant to them.

A realisation of a new presence of his wife came to him as he listened to the words of a down-and-out he met as he sat with his thoughts in St Stephen's Green. They shared their stories and as they parted the man said to him the prophetic words, 'The seed in your heart shall blossom.' It was only gradually that he came to realise the truth of these words in the mysterious presence that emerged from the memory of the relationship he shared with Olive. In this memory of their abiding love he realised his life was blossoming 'wonderfully and beautifully and that it would continue to blossom'.

The way John found his wife present to him in a new way after her death is very like the new and mysterious way Jesus became present to his disciples after his death. When two of them met him on the road to Emmaus they were so overcome by their loss that they did not recognise him. It was only as they listened to him as 'he talked to them on the road, while he opened to them the scriptures' that they became convinced that it was Jesus who was with them and as a result their 'hearts burned' within them. However, it was in the memory of his love of them 'to the end' in 'the breaking of bread' that they recognised he would be with them always and in a way more real for them than when he first called them. (Lk 24:13-35)

CHAPTER 8

The Christian as essentially a listener

In this chapter we reflect on the importance of being receptive or of listening to what Jesus reveals to us at Mass and on how we can go about this.

Listening to the good times

When John Quinn's wife died he was initially engulfed in a sea of loss. He had no alternative but to go back over the story of her death, to walk around in and to surrender to the terrible reality of her absence. With time he was able to move out of this sea of loss and towards the sea of love as he remembered the good times they had together and as he put words on the love that emerged from this side of their story. Through being able to listen to the story of their life together a picture of Olive emerged and became increasingly real. What was basic to this emergence of her love was John Quinn's ability to listen, to put words on this love and to savour it.

I was at a boarding school for 9 years and in such enclosed circumstances and over such a long period I got to know some of my companions very well. I remember them now by the nicknames many of them had. As I recall some of these, I am amazed at how perceptive they were and at how imaginatively they were expressed. A new boy or teacher would not be long in the school before he was given a nickname which stuck with him for the rest of his time there. I remember one boy whom we called Rashers because he always looked so well-fed at a time, just after the Second World War, when our diet left most of us looking scrawny. Another boy was called Currant Bun because he had more than his share of adolescent pimples. Then there was a stocky but pale boy who had jet black hair who was called The Badger.

This capacity to capture something distinctive about others in a telling word or phrase reveals an intuitive gift we all have. Though we recognise this gift in others we may not realise that we too have it and use it all the time. We admire this gift in poets, the skill they have to notice and share with us in a striking way the deep meaning they find in the ordinary. They have, to a marked degree, the ability to listen to the extraordinary things that ordinary people and circumstances reveal to us and to express these in a creative way.

The neglected poet in us

Unfortunately, the development of this intuitive gift has been a low priority in our educational system. During my years as a teacher I became aware of how little attention was given to developing the gift which our senses, our intuition and our feelings are. We have as a result an underdeveloped ability to listen to reality with our heart, with our soul and with our senses. Subjects like Religious Education and literature, history and geography that seek to cultivate these abilities were treated as unimportant compared to subjects like science and mathematics that developed our capacity to think logically. These more cerebral subjects also had the practical merit that 'they got people jobs' when they left school.

It was when I became a teacher in the school of reflection and prayer that I noticed how poorly people are served by our educational system. The two things I found people had most difficulty with when they wanted to learn to reflect and pray were firstly making space for these and secondly developing their capacity to listen. People prefer to think about the Word than to listen to what it reveals about Jesus and the way he embodies God's love for us. It is very significant that in the whole of the New Testament the one thing that God specifically asks us to do is to listen to Jesus.

Then from the cloud came a voice that said, 'This is my Son, my Chosen; listen to him!' (Lk 9:35)

'Listen to him!'

At the heart of what we believe is the reality that the three persons of the Trinity want to reveal themselves to us. This makes the Christian essentially a listener. If we want to enter fully into this role, the first thing we need to do is to distinguish listening from thinking. When we hear a passage of scripture we tend to *think*, to be active as we work out its meaning and then its implications for the way we live. Thus, when we think about the Word of God we tend to work out what we are called to do for God rather than listen to what God wants to do for us. On the other hand, when we *listen* to the Word we are receptive to what the three persons wish to reveal about themselves, to the 'good news' of their love for us, and our lovableness in their eyes.

When Jesus invites us to listen to the Word of God he is not asking us to think about the meaning of a story in the gospels or about its implications for the way we live. Rather, he asks us to be aware of, to put words on and to savour the glimpse he gives us of his love and of our lovableness. Listening also includes our ability to repeatedly dwell with the glimpses of his love which he gives us so that they are converted into the convictions in which faith consists. In his parable about the Sower, Jesus highlights this vital role of listening when he invites us not only to listen to or 'hear the Word' but to 'hold it fast' as well. This is what is necessary if the Word is to take root in us and to grow to maturity.

> But as for that in the good soil, these are the ones who, when they hear the word, hold it fast in an honest and good heart, and bear fruit with patient endurance. (Lk 8:15)

Listening to the word results not only in our growth to maturity but in the intimacy and happiness that comes with this maturity.

> My mother and my brothers are those who hear the word of God and do it. ... Happy rather are those who hear the word of God and obey it! (Lk 8:19-21, 11:27-28)

The basic response to Grace

We can judge how important listening is at Mass by our own de-
sires when we give people a gift. We would like them to look at
and appreciate it before voicing any other response. But even
more than appreciating the gift we want them to listen to what
we are saying to them through the gift. In the light of this experience we need to ask ourselves whether the same is true for the
three persons of the Trinity when they give us the gift of themselves in complete self-disclosure. When at Mass Jesus gives us
the gift not only of all he has but of himself, what response does
he want? Would he like us first to contemplate his gift, to ponder
and appreciate it, before we seek words to thank him or before
we decide what we can give him in return? The Martha and
Mary story has a lot to say to us in answer to this question. The
fact that Mary sat and listened to Jesus was seen by him as 'the
better part' compared to the way Martha responded to him with
her service.

> Now as they went on their way, he entered a certain village,
> where a woman named Martha welcomed him into her home.
> She had a sister named Mary, *who sat at the Lord's feet and lis-
> tened to what he was saying.* But Martha was distracted by her
> many tasks; so she came to him and asked, 'Lord, do you not
> care that my sister has left me to do all the work by myself?
> Tell her then to help me.' But the Lord answered her, 'Martha,
> Martha, you are worried and distracted by many things; there
> is need of only one thing. Mary has chosen *the better part*,
> which will not be taken away from her.' (Lk 10:38-42)

The contention of this chapter is that the basic thing Jesus wants
us to do at Mass is to listen. This moment, when we allow ourselves time to be attentive, receptive and appreciative is the primary response that Mass invites. What often works against our
adopting this contemplative approach to Mass is our tendency
to identify love primarily with desire, with being active and
with service. This receptive stance is what Jesus invites us to
adopt in chapter 6 of John's gospel where he asks us to 'eat the

bread of life'. Here the word 'bread' stands for both the Word of God and Jesus' body and blood. The word 'eat' stands for all the steps we need to take if we are to savour and delight in the love which the bread symbolises.

A difficulty worth overcoming

The difficulty of listening to what Jesus reveals to us at Mass is formidable but it is worth overcoming. What makes listening difficult is our well-established tendency to think and talk rather than to listen. People who listen to our story, and rather than interrupting draw us out, are rare. Our reluctance to listen is strengthened by the excessively active culture in which we live and by the way we were educated to think and to be assertive rather than to listen and be receptive. Listening is also difficult because it involves putting aside our own concerns and focusing on being receptive to those of others.

Nevertheless, learning to listen is worth the effort involved for on it depends the health of three important areas of the Christian life. Listening is first of all the foundation of conversation. If we do not listen, the other element of conversation, our emotional response, ceases to be genuine or honest. This is because our emotions are our heart's response to the reality we open ourselves to by listening. If our emotions are not aroused, listened to and shared, they become dormant and our ability to communicate is seriously impaired. Secondly, without this conversation or communication, of which listening is the most important part, our relationships lose what keeps them healthy. In other words, the quality of the way we relate with God and with each other depends on the quality of our listening. Thirdly, if we do not develop our ability to listen, prayer, understood as listening and responding to the revelation of God's love, becomes impossible.

Mass, which is built around the desire of the three persons of the Trinity to reveal themselves to us, is ultimately a listening experience. The three key moments of the Mass, the readings, the consecration and the communion, reflect this reality. We are invited to listen to the readings as God's Word or self-revelation, to listen to what is said to us at the consecration about Jesus loving us 'to death' and to savour this love at the time of communion.

Some suggestions for reflection and prayer
1. Read the following story a few times and then see what it is saying to you about listening, about its difficulty, and about how you overcome this.

> *Listening to the bells:*
> There was once a famous monastery that was built on a small island a few miles from the mainland. In time the island sank below the water and with it the monastery. People, however, still came to visit the place, to listen to the bells which could be heard by pilgrims who really listened.
> There was one man who came to hear these bells and sat for days on the shore listening as best he could. In the end he decided to go home but before he left, he lay down on the shore and relaxed just watching the clouds. Then, as he lay there completely relaxed and lost in wonder at the beauty of the clouds, he heard the bells. Ever after he could hear the bells when he wanted to.

2. Tell the story of yourself as a listener. For example, when you were a child, were you assigned the role of a listener, were you to be seen and not heard. Now that you are an adult are the roles reversed? Do you have any relationship in which you are by choice mainly a listener?

3. There is a side of each of us that is receptive, contemplative and wants to listen. There is also a responsive, assertive, active side of us that needs to react and talk. Outline the story of yourself as a listener and then say how you see this more contemplative and receptive side of yourself now. Enter a dialogue between these two sides of yourself, writing down a few statements you each make in this dialogue.

4. Reflect prayerfully on any of the following pieces of scripture in the light of what has come up for you in 1-3 above: Gen 28:10-22, Gen 32:23-33, 1 Sam 3:10, Lk 9:35, Lk 8:15.

CHAPTER 9

A prayer of praise and thanksgiving

In chapter 8 we saw the role listening plays in our being receptive to the love revealed to us at Mass. In this chapter we look at
the response which the feelings aroused by listening calls for.

The intimacy emotional honesty leads to
As John Quinn remembers and listens to what the story of his
life with Olive says to him, he becomes aware of and shares
with us a sea of feelings. The pain of loss arouses feelings of
intense sadness that death had taken her away in such an ultimate way. But there are also the feelings of joy and even delight in the memory of so many good times together. There
are feelings he describes that are almost unbearably poignant,
such as those of appreciation, gratitude and warmth, embedded in his memory of his life with Olive. As we listen to him
we have no doubt that noticing and naming his feelings is a
most effective way of dwelling with and savouring the love
they shared and thus of finding her present in a new way.

In my lifetime there has been a revolution in the way we relate
with our feelings. In the 50s we were given to believe that they
did not count, then in the 70s they became all important. Since
then they have tended to assume their indispensable role in the
way we relate. Feelings have gone from being peripheral to
being all-important and then to playing their crucial part in the
way we communicate.

When I entered the seminary in 1953, doing God's will was
the objective set before us and our feelings were seen to be irrelevant to carrying this out. We were expected to obey the rules of
the seminary as the practical expression of God's will and our

personal feelings were given little or no part to play in this. In our studies, feelings were ignored as being too subjective and too complex to sort out. Later when I heard the saying, 'Feelings don't count', used to describe the status of feelings in the 50s I felt it captured my experience of a time when there was an almost complete disregard of how we felt. What was considered important was that our thoughts and actions conformed to a set standard and our feelings were not meant to get in the way of this conformity.

Then in the 60s and 70s relationships and how people felt within them became all-important. How people felt became the accepted criterion for what they said and did, so that feelings assumed a central role in determining what was true and what was good. Since the 70s people have discovered a middle ground between the extremes of the 50s and 60s. Feelings are allowed to play their crucial role in relationships and in the communication that goes on within them. Feelings are seen to be central to healthy relationships, to how we respond to others by sharing our feelings with them. This sharing, however, makes demands on us as it requires that we develop our capacity to notice our feelings and to express them.

The role feelings play in the Mass

To understand the crucial role feelings play in the Mass we need to examine the role our feelings play in our relationships and especially in the way we communicate within these. In other words, the development of our relationships depends on our ability to listen to others and on our ability to express how we feel about what they have said to us. If what we listen to is as dramatic as the revelation made to us at Mass, it is bound to arouse strong feelings. We need to become aware of these and to find an authentic way of expressing them in the prayers which form such a large part of the Mass.

There are two levels of feeling involved in the way we relate with Jesus in the Mass. There is the emotional level with which we normally associate the word feelings, but there is also what we might call the convictional level of feeling, which is much deeper. At this deeper level are found our values or our convictions about what is truly worthwhile in life. These are the things we feel most deeply about, the things we could not imagine ourselves living without and they have a profound influence on what we feel at the emotional level.

Positive and negative feelings
What people say to us will usually arouse a mixture of positive and negative feeling. What we hear will make us feel good or bad or, more often, a subtle mixture of the two. To deal with these two kinds of feeling in a healthy way, we need to become more aware of our feelings and of the best way of dealing with them. If we take the trouble to notice and put words on our positive feelings we intensify them and add a new dimension to our relationships. If we notice and name our negative feelings we will gradually free ourselves from the way they tend to dominate us.

Some of the feelings we refer to as positive are stirred up by the extraordinary love the Mass keeps us in touch with. These feelings, such as a sense of wonder and appreciation, of joy and gratitude, are aroused by all the love we have already received. But there is also the hope and the desire, the courage and the enthusiasm aroused by the abundance of life and happiness that Mass reminds us may yet be ours. We also bring to Mass a body of negative feeling that is as deadening as the positive feeling is enlivening. These negative feelings may include a sense of heaviness or indifference, a sense of guilt and its accompanying sadness. As we look towards the future we may be dominated by anxiety, by restlessness and by a lack of hope.

Preventing negative feelings from dominating
It is a strange fact about human nature that we are drawn to dwell with our negative feelings more than with our positive ones. If we do not develop a strategy for dealing with this tendency of the negative to dominate, it can colour the way we see

ourselves. This negative way of seeing ourselves can in turn prevent us from hearing and believing the hugely positive things that are said to us at Mass.

If we are to be free to hear and to savour the positive things the Mass reveals to us, it is important to befriend the dark companion we all live with. Rather than try to banish this dark side of ourselves, that turns up in feelings like frustration, guilt and sadness, we need to befriend it. We can do this by accepting our own dark side as just a small part of an otherwise good self. This acceptance, whether it takes the form of forgiveness, tolerance, walking contentedly or even humorously with all that is deficient in us, will gradually release us from the dominance of our negative feelings.

Cultivating positive feelings

The purpose of freeing ourselves from negative feelings is that we may focus our attention on and cultivate the good feelings that what we remember at Mass keeps us in touch with. Once we become more familiar with these feelings we are in a better position to identify with the sentiments expressed in the prayers of the Mass. It is hard to get away from the experience that the prayers we say at Mass are created for another time and place. If we experience them in this way, we do not easily identify and resonate with them. To make these prayers of the Mass more our own, or more a response that is heartfelt, we need to do two things. We need to get in touch with feelings such as gratitude that are aroused by what we remember at Mass, and to get in touch too with how the prayers of the Mass express these feelings.

To get in touch with the feelings Mass can arouse we need to explore the range and depth of our own feelings. One such feeling is the wonder stirred up when we remember at Mass how much we are loved and how Jesus invites us to 'eat' or abide in this love. Out of this wonder comes feelings of appreciation and the desire to celebrate and to praise. Other feelings that are aroused by Jesus' extraordinary generosity at Mass are gratitude and the courage and joy that hope gives.

Renewing the way we say the prayers of the Mass

To be meaningful, the prayers of the Mass must be seen as the second phase of the dialogue which the Mass essentially is. If they are not said as an expression of the feelings generated by the greatest expression of love the world has ever known, then they will not be as authentic and engaging as they ought. In our effort to get in touch with how the prayers of the Mass express our feelings in an authentic and engaging way, it is important first of all to notice how much of the Mass is spent saying prayers. For example, there are the prayers surrounding the readings, the offertory, the consecration and the communion. Even though the prayers of the Mass are more formal than the Psalms, they share their capacity to express a great range and depth of feeling. For example, there is a very explicit expression of powerful feelings, such as gratitude, appreciation, joy and desire, expressed in the Gloria, the Psalm, the Preface and the Holy, Holy.

Something that would make the prayers of the Mass more authentic and engaging is a prayerful, personal perusal of each of them. This would involve taking time to become aware of the sentiments expressed in each of these prayers and of the words and images used to express these sentiments. Even though these prayers come from another time and place, their depth and beauty are perennial. The Mass as the supreme expression of Jesus' love is our greatest work of art. It is worth taking the time it needs to unfold the beautiful way this work of art has been expressed. Like other works of art, any time we give to perusing what the Mass says to us, and how it says this, will reward us richly.

If we enter into the prayers of the Mass in ways like these they can become an engaging way of responding to the profound love revealed to us afresh in every Mass. Thus the Mass can become the best way not only of renewing our vision of God's love but of cultivating feelings such as the 'complete' joy that abiding in this love leads to. (Jn 15:9-11)

A full range and depth of feeling
We will end this chapter with some examples of how a variety of
our feelings are expressed in the prayers of the Mass. For example, the following words are part of most of the prefaces said at
Mass.

> Father, all-powerful and ever-living God
> we do well always and everywhere to give you thanks
> through Jesus Christ our Lord.

The following words at the end of the Preface as well as those of
the Gloria could be said as a formal expression of reverence or as
a cry of ecstasy.

> Holy, holy, holy Lord, God of power and might,
> heaven and earth are full of your glory.
> Hosanna in the highest.
> Blessed is he who comes in the name of the Lord.
> Hosanna in the highest.

In the prayers of the Mass we 'sing the new song of creation':

> Earth unites with heaven
> to sing the new song of creation
> as we adore and praise you for ever.
> *(Preface of Holy Eucharist II)*

Some suggestions for reflection and prayer
1. Read the following quotations and see what they say to you
about the stance you adopt towards your feelings.

> We are governed more by our feelings than by reason. Events
> that exercise those feelings will produce wonderful effects.
> (*S. Adams*)

> When feelings are very strong, affective prayer is possible,
> only if the person can put them before the Lord and let him
> accept them. Otherwise, the unnoticed negative feelings will
> stand like a ridge between him and the Holy One.
> (*The Practice of Spiritual Direction*, Connolly and Barry)

I have owed to them,
In hours of weariness, sensations sweet,
Felt in the blood, and felt along the heart;
And passing even into my purer mind,
With tranquil restoration: feelings too
Of unremembered pleasure: such, perhaps,
As have no slight or trivial influence
On that best portion of a good man's life;
His little, nameless, unremembered acts
Of kindness and of love ...
(William Wordsworth)

2. Tell the story of the emergence of your feelings as an import-ant element in your relationships. For example, describe when you first became aware of the importance of your feelings and how you see their role in your life now.

3. Relax in a place you like to be on your own. Let Jesus join you and after you have greeted one another let him ask you how you feel and then ask him how he feels.

4. Choose one of the prayers of the Mass you like and say it slowly a few times to let the feelings it expresses emerge. Reflect prayerfully on any of the following pieces of scripture in the light of anything you have got from 1-3 above: Jer 31:3, Jn 15:9-11, Lk 10:21-22, Lk 19:41.

CHAPTER 10

Repent and believe the good news

In chapters 8 and 9 we examined how we 'abide in' or immerse our whole person in the love we remember at Mass by listening and responding to it. In this chapter we focus on how, by listening and responding to Jesus' love revealed at Mass, we can answer the essential call of the gospel to 'repent and believe the good news'.

A new mysterious presence

Before the end of the story John Quinn tells us, we realise that he has learned to live with a new sense of his wife's love and presence. He has done this by savouring and making his own of the glimpses of her he is given as he tells the story of their life together. The glimpses of her love and all that this means for him have become convictions, convictions not only about what was true or authentic about her but about how attractive, good and even how beautiful she was and is for him. These convictions create a strong sense of her presence, a presence that is as real as her physical presence was for him when she was alive, even though it is much more mysterious. In this new way she has become present, he realises that his life is blossoming 'wonderfully and beautifully and that it would continue to blossom'.

Recently I read A. N. Wilson's life of Hilaire Belloc. What struck me about Belloc was the clarity he had about what he believed in and about what was important for him. In the 150 books he wrote we are never left in any doubt about what he considered was true and what was worthwhile, about his vision and his values. Even though I know that like him I live out of a vision and

value system that I have built up over a life-time, I find it difficult to visit and articulate this deepest area of myself.

The emergence of a vision
When I examine *the vision* that has emerged for me over the
years, two ways of looking at it emerge. One of these looks at
this vision as an exterior knowledge that is intellectual and abstract, the other looks at it as an interior knowledge that is experiential and down to earth. The exterior knowledge was my quest
for most of my life as I sought an all-inclusive picture of how all
the different parts of my vision of life fitted together. It was as if
life presented me with a giant jig-saw puzzle and I had to put all
the pieces in place if I was to see the big picture. I believed this
was necessary if I was to discover the design or the all-inclusive
vision that would emerge when all the pieces were in place.
However, it never did emerge and I now realise that the reason
is that life is mysterious and understanding it fully in this intellectual way is beyond us. There are always pieces of the jig-saw
puzzle left over that will not fit in and probably never will.

It was only recently when someone who teaches Philosophy
asked me what my philosophy of life was that I realised I had
left this intellectual quest aside to make room for another. When
I reflected on this I realised that another kind of vision had
emerged along the way and replaced the one I associate with my
student years. I cannot say when it began to emerge but I knew I
had moved house when I came across and was captivated by
Henri de Lubac's statement that 'enlightenment is not an idea
but what we see in another's eyes'. I realised that the vision I
was now living out of and that gave everything meaning for me
was one I saw in Jesus' eyes. It was also a vision of myself as acknowledged, accepted and affirmed by him. This vision found
expression when I wrote the book *Nine Portraits* and it is a vision
of Jesus that enthrals me with its truth, its goodness and its
beauty.

The growth of a value system

The value system that I came across in my study of ethics and moral theology was intellectually complex, legalistic and lacking in colour and attractiveness. Even though I am not sure when another value system emerged and took over from this one, I am aware that this has happened and in a way parallel to how the vision I now live out of emerged. What is central to this new value system is the love of Jesus, especially his love of us 'to the utmost extent'. This love is expressed in his passion, death and resurrection, and at Mass in his body 'given up' for us and in his blood 'shed' for us. The more we learn to believe in his love the more lovable or valuable we discover ourselves, others and all of creation to be. Jesus' commandment that we love others as he has loved us is at the centre of our value system. (Jn 15:12)

The way Jesus' vision and value system becomes ours is when in answer to his invitation, 'Come and see', we get to know him in the gospel stories. From what Jesus says and does in these stories we get glimpses of him and, if we make our own of these, a vision of him and of his attractiveness builds up. This vision of what Jesus calls the good news is of a world pervaded by the love and providence of God. It is a vision of all that is true, good and beautiful.

Repenting in order to believe

Belief in this vision calls for repentance. This is a radical change of mind and heart, of vision and values, of the way we see and feel about the world around us. This change of mind and heart involves letting go of old ways of seeing ourselves and others that are at variance with what Jesus asks us to believe in. For example, if we see the world as a hostile place, our vision is at variance with the world pervaded by God's love and providence that Jesus asks us to believe in. This repentance, or letting go of distorted ways of seeing Jesus and ourselves so that we may believe in Jesus' love and our lovableness in his eyes, is the essential call of the gospel. It is at the heart of the Christian vocation.

> Now after John was arrested, Jesus came to Galilee, pro-
> claiming the good news of God, and saying, 'The time is ful-
> filled, and the kingdom of God has come near; repent, and
> believe in the good news.' (Mk 1:15)

The Christian vocation is to go on a journey in which we leave
behind a distorted vision of reality in order to arrive at the one
Jesus invites us to believe in. This leaving of old ways of seeing
things that are familiar and comfortable is painful and is compared by Jesus to 'dying'. It is, however, like the dying of the
seed which is the condition of new life emerging and coming to
fruition.

> Very truly, I tell you, unless a grain of wheat falls into the
> earth and dies, it remains just a single grain; but if it dies, it
> bears much fruit. (Jn 12:24)

The offertory of the Mass is our ongoing commitment to enter
into the death and resurrection of Jesus, to die with him by answering his call to repentance and to rise with him by answering
his call to believe in his love. There is a sacrifice at the heart of
this repentance, or this dying to our old self, that the offertory
prayers refer to.

> Lord God, we ask you to receive us
> and be pleased with this sacrifice we offer you
> with humble and contrite hearts.
> *(Prayer of offering)*

Listening and responding to the Word

The most effective way we can bring about this change of mind
and heart that belief calls for is through listening and then responding to God's self-revelation in the Word and especially in
the Mass. This form of conversational prayer has been seen from
the time of St Augustine to be basic to the Christian life. It is
based on what Jesus says is necessary if the seed or the Word is
to take root in us and reach maturity. He says we must *listen* to
the Word of God and '*hold it fast* in an honest and good heart,
and bear fruit with patient endurance'. (Lk 8:15)

If the offering of the Mass is our commitment to answer the

essential call of the gospel to repent and believe and if prayer is the most effective way of doing this, then the commitment to pray is an essential part of the offering of the Mass. The prayer involved here is the conversational kind that involves the kind of listening and responding that we have looked at in chapters 8 and 9. It is the prayer initiated by God's self-revelation in the Word and in the 'breaking of the bread'. This kind of prayer that we commit ourselves to in the offertory of the Mass needs to become more a part of the life of every Christian than it has been. This is the conviction that Dr Liam Ryan, professor of sociology at Maynooth, voiced in an article he wrote in *The Furrow* in 1983. In it he expresses his belief that the prayer element in the church has to become as much a pastoral priority as the institutional and intellectual elements if our faith is to remain healthy.

The need for a catalyst
Making the space for prayer and learning its skills is something we find very hard to do today. If we are to face these difficulties and undertake the discipline of prayer we need a catalyst. This for the Christian is the attractiveness of Jesus and of the love he essentially is and that we are a hunger for. It was this essential attractiveness of Jesus that drew his first disciples to him in such a powerful way that they 'left everything' to be with him. It is this essential attractiveness that Jesus spoke about in his parables about the treasure and the pearl. In these he compares the attractiveness of his love to that of the treasure and the priceless pearl for which we will pay any price. If through prayer, we become aware of the attractiveness of his love, of its overwhelming goodness and beauty, we will do anything that is necessary to attain it.

> The kingdom of heaven is like a merchant in search of fine pearls; on finding one pearl of great value, he went and sold all that he had and bought it. (Mt 13:44-46)

It is in the Mass that we see the full extent and depth of the attractiveness of Jesus' love in that we experience it to be 'to the utmost extent'. Here his love reaches its climax and creates a magnetic field in which everything is drawn into a new order centring on him. (Jn 12:32)

Establishing this new order
We will conclude this chapter by looking at some of the ways we use at Mass to express our willingness to undertake the change of mind and heart that belief in Jesus' love of us calls for. This willingness finds expression chiefly in the offertory. In it we commit ourselves to extend and deepen our belief in Jesus' love and in our own lovableness in his eyes. But so far as the offertory is a call to believe in our own lovableness, it is also a call to believe in that of others and of all creation. Thus the offertory is closely associated with *the bidding prayers*. These are a day to day expression of the concerns that loving others as Jesus has loved us urge us to include.

Before we hear the Word *we trace a cross on our head, lips and heart*. In this gesture we symbolise our desire to let the Word of God we are about to hear influence the way we think, feel and speak. By this gesture we express our desire that by listening to the Word of God and by finding words to respond to what we hear we may change our minds and hearts.

In the prayers of offering we express our belief in the overwhelming truth that through eating the bread and drinking the wine that we offer we may 'come to share in the divinity of Christ'.

By the mystery of this water and wine,
may we come to share in the divinity of Christ
who humbled himself to share in our humanity.
(Prayer of offering)

Some suggestions for reflection and prayer
1   What do the following story and quotation say to you about the offertory of the Mass?

The Crab's Shell
There is a certain kind of crab that lives in a shell but not the

one shell for life. As it grows it must discard the old shell that it has outgrown or it will die. Changing shells is not easy for the old one has to be split open and the crab becomes very vulnerable until a new one has grown. When its shell becomes too thick, too tough to crack open, the crab cannot grow any more. That is when it dies.

Our shells are not as visible as those of the crab but they are as real. Our shells are formed by years of habit. There are shells developed to protect us against others, shells that are shaped by the roles we play as parents or children, as employer or employee. Life is all the time inviting us to change our shell, to risk feeling vulnerable when, in order to grow, we shed what we have outgrown. The alternative is that we hold on to our shell until it becomes so thick that we cannot crack it or grow within it. We may be dead long before we die.

As host and cup will be transformed into Christ's body and blood, so we should intend to offer to God our very selves, that our lives may be transformed into what he wants them to be.

(Our Splendid Eucharist, Raymond Moloney)

2. Assuming that you have not always understood the offertory of the Mass in the same way as you do now, describe a few key times in your life when your understanding of the offertory developed.

3. Enter your inner room and after being quiet there for a short while let Jesus join you. He asks you about the thoughts and feelings that arise for you when you think about the offertory of the Mass. For example, he may ask you about what you feel drawn to offer as your part of the offertory. You might ask him if he finds what you offer pleases him. As you reflect on this experience, after Jesus has left you, see whether you have found yourself accepted and affirmed by him or not.

4. Reflect prayerfully on any of the following pieces of scripture in the light of what has emerged for you in 1-3 above: Deut 30:15-20, Mt 7:13-14, Jn 10:10, Lk 10:25-28, Mk 1:14-15.

CHAPTER 11

The change of mind and heart suffering can effect

In chapter 10 we examined how by listening and responding to the good news presented to us at Mass we can answer Jesus' call to 'repent and believe the good news'. In this chapter we examine how life's sufferings can also challenge us to answer this same call.

The light we see only in the darkness
It is only in the darkness of separation that we may realise fully the true value and beauty of those we love. Even temporary separation forces us to realise how much it means to have those we love around us, to glimpse how indispensable they are to our happiness. With death this separation seems initially to be absolute. This was the experience of John Quinn when his wife died. However, her death forced him not only to face the terrible pain of losing her but it invited him to see in perspective her role in his life. With the emergence of this perspective came a mysterious new presence which he was led to see as a final blossoming of their relationship.

This new way John Quinn's wife became present to him after her death is very like the mysterious new way Jesus became present to his disciples after his death. When two of his disciples met him on the road to Emmaus they were so overcome by their loss that they did not initially recognise this new way he was present to them. It was only as they listened to him as 'he talked to them on the road, while he opened to them the scriptures' that they became convinced that he was present to them in a more profound and permanent way than ever before. The evidence for this is the way that their 'hearts burned' within them as he spoke to them on the way. However, it was the memory of his love of them 'to the end' or in 'the breaking of bread' that they recognised he would be with them always and in a way more real than when he first called them. (Lk 24:13-36)

Two roads diverged in a yellow wood
When I was in my early forties I wrote a letter to each member of my family about a decision I was making. I prefaced the letter with a quotation from Dante: 'In the middle of my years I find myself in a dark wood, the way ahead not clear.' I think some of my family were alarmed at these words, maybe taking them too literally. Perhaps, they thought that I was in crisis, that I had lost a sense of where my life was going. Now, while I was not in crisis in this sense, it was as if I had come to a divide in the road where I felt drawn to leave the well mapped road I was travelling. This decision was necessary if I was to take the road less travelled even though it was not clear where it would take me. From that time on, the concluding lines of Robert Frost's poem, *The Road Less Travelled*, have had great appeal for me.

Two roads diverged in a yellow wood
And I took the one less travelled
And that has made all the difference.

At the time I was invited to make my decision I had moved from southern Zambia to a town in the north called Kitwe, from teaching at secondary level to lecturing in a teacher's training college. It was a dramatic change for me. Till then I had been a member of a big community living in a district where people were friendly and where I was very caught up in my life as a teacher. During the six years I was in that place I was extremely busy writing text books around the areas of Religious Education, English language and literature that I was involved in teaching. When I moved to Kitwe all that changed. There were just three of us in the community and the work I was doing, though important, did not engage me in the creative way my previous work had. I felt I was living on the fringe of things with little creative challenge in the work I was doing. I became conscious that the way ahead was not clear. It was as if I had come to a roadblock and was being forced to take a dirt road that led into the bush. I was being taken off in a new direction and it was not clear where I was going. I felt I was like the people in the Exodus story when they lost their way and wandered around in circles.

In hindsight that experience of darkness or of being 'in a dark wood' was a time when I was forced to review, re-evaluate and reorientate my life. Looking back on the period of frenetic activity that had preceded my going to Kitwe I realise the truth of what a relative of mine said to my brother during a very busy period of his life, 'A time will come when you will no longer hear the birds.' Perhaps, I needed to confront the fact that I had been so busy that I was no longer listening to the birds.

In reviewing this experience I now see that, in terms of the story of Martha and Mary, I was being given time to let the more contemplative side of myself find its rightful place in my life. I was being urged to make the space to sit like Mary at the feet of Jesus and listen to him, to adopt the contemplative stance to life that Jesus calls the 'one thing necessary'. (Lk 10:42) The catalyst that helped me make this shift in my priorities was someone who at that time came to me looking for guidance. However, as things worked out she was the one who gave me a new sense of direction. In an indirect way she taught me that life is more about relationships than work, more about Grace than anything I might achieve through my own effort. In other words, she invited me to set out on an inner journey, one that I have been engaged in ever since.

Grace grows best in Winter
What I notice as I look back on the dark periods of my life is how much they taught me. I am convinced that dark periods, when hardships, sufferings and humiliations put us in touch with our limitations and weaknesses, can be times of great growth. Perhaps they have more potential for growth than periods when we feel creative and in control. Times of darkness ask us who

and what we believe in. They challenge and even confront us with bringing out into the open how we see and feel about what matters most. Life's hardships put us up against the wall as it were and ask us, 'Do you really believe in a provident God?', one who leads you 'in the fire by night, and in the cloud by day, to show you the route you should take'? (Deut 1:29-33)

We prefer the familiar and the comfortable, whether it is a road, a relationship or a way we see and feel about people and events. We are reluctant to relinquish old ways of seeing people and events and the way we feel about them. It is as if we struggle to find a new way only when the old one is blocked and it often takes the shock of suffering to jolt us out of the groove we have settled into. We tend to become set in our ways so that we stop growing in our relationships and it takes a dramatic happening to help us break out of the confined area we have got used to living in.

Ways of approaching suffering

When confronted by difficult relationships or situations we may decide to take refuge in flight from the pain these cause. We may refuse to deal with these situations by denying that they exist or we may just postpone dealing with them until we have no alternative but to face them. Again, we may decide to fight or wrestle with these situations, relying on our own resources to get the better of them. However, since so many situations which cause us to suffer are outside our control, we will experience a lot of frustration when we seek to handle them on our own.

Another way of dealing with suffering is put before us at Mass when it invites us to see our suffering in perspective. Initially, we tend to see our sufferings in terms of what we have lost, what we have been deprived of. But gradually, we may come to see what we have been deprived of in the broader context of all the good that is ours. If we view life from the perspective of the full extent and depth of Jesus' love that Mass puts us in touch with, then life's darkness can lead to an increased sense of this love. The renewed sense of being loved in this way can make our hearts burn with joy and enthusiasm in the way it did with the two disciples Jesus met on the road to Emmaus.

> They said to each other, 'Were not our hearts burning within us while he was talking to us on the road, while he was opening the scriptures to us? (Lk 24:32)

The experience of dark times causes a crisis. It confronts us with taking one of two ways, a constructive way that challenges us with difficult changes, or a destructive way we tend to drift down because it seems the easier alternative. In his parable of the two ways Jesus says that few take the way to life. Is this because coming to know Jesus and accepting his vision and his values involves committing ourselves to a difficult change of mind and heart? (Mt 7:13-14)

'The road that leads to destruction'
There are three stages on the road 'to destruction' which we need to be aware of so that we can discern the unhealthy influence of each of them.

* The first stage takes the form of the strong negative feelings that surface when we go through difficult times. We will notice, for example, frustration surfacing when a relationship or a work we are involved in does not turn out as we had expected. This frustration can colour our day, diminishing much that is good so that we hear ourselves saying, 'That was a bad day.'

* We move to the second stage if we do not deal with our negative feelings. If feelings such as anger or guilt persist they colour the way we see ourselves. In this way ugly feelings can generate a poor image of ourselves or emphasise one that is already there.

* The third stage occurs when this poor self-image makes it hard to believe others when they affirm us. This erosion of belief in ourselves makes it more difficult for us to believe in the good news Jesus wants us to renew at Mass. From the

ease with which we drift down this road to 'destruction' we can see why Jesus says that many people take it. (Mt 7:13-14)

'The road that leads to life'
In times when we travel through the valley of darkness, the faith that this darkness challenges us to get in touch with, leads to life. The reason is that at the core of this faith that the Mass seeks to enliven is the fact that we are loved and lovable to the utmost extent. (Jn 13:1) If we absorb it, nothing is as life-giving as this love of Jesus that sacrifices all for each of us. (Gal 2:10) It is in the Mass that this love is given its strongest expression and that we are also given a way of absorbing it.

We see how in practice Jesus led the two disciples he met on the road to Emmaus to see their sufferings in a life-giving way. By means of the Word of God and the 'breaking of bread' he led them from a negative way of seeing their suffering to a more positive one. As a result, their feelings of sadness about the past and despair about the future are changed into feelings of joy and enthusiasm. There are three stages in the way Jesus leads these two disciples and us to turn their suffering into this life-giving experience.

Stage 1
The first stage involves Jesus accompanying us with the same sensitivity and compassion as he accompanied his two disciples on the road to Emmaus. He asks us, as he did them, to tell him about the events that make us downcast. Then by listening to us tell our story he acknowledges us as worthy of his full attention. People who listen to us at a time when we are low acknowledge our significance for them and restore our confidence in ourselves.

> While they were talking and discussing, Jesus himself came near and went with them ... And he said to them, 'What are you discussing with each other while you walk along?' They stood still, looking sad. Then one of them, whose name was Cleopas, answered him, 'Are you the only stranger in

Jerusalem who does not know the things that have taken place there in these days?' He asked them, 'What things?' (Lk 24:15-19)

Stage 2

Jesus helps us to accept our sufferings and the weak side of ourselves that emerges when we suffer. He does this by putting our sufferings in perspective, helping us to understand that our sufferings have a place in God's plan. (Rom 8:28) By listening to what we are going through, in the way he listens to and draws out his two disciples on the road to Emmaus, Jesus leads us to believe that he takes our sufferings seriously. He accepts us where we are and does not trivialise what we are going through. The fact that Jesus accepts and identifies with the weaknesses and temptations that occur when we suffer (Heb 4:14-15) can lead to our accepting and even living contentedly with the suffering that is part of every life.

Then beginning with Moses and all the prophets, he interpreted to them the things about himself in all the scriptures. As they came near the village to which they were going, he walked ahead as if he were going on. But they urged him strongly, saying, 'Stay with us, because it is almost evening and the day is now nearly over.' So he went in to stay with them. (Lk 24:25-29)

Stage 3

When the limitations that life's hardships put us in touch with are accepted, we become more open to Jesus' appreciation of how heroic we are in times like these. The high point of Jesus' appreciation of us is found in the Mass when he reveals to us that we are loved, and in his eyes lovable, to an extraordinary degree. This reality, confirmed by the Word and 'the breaking of the bread' at Mass, is what makes our hearts too burn with enthusiasm and joy.

They said to each other, 'Were not our hearts burning within us while he was talking to us on the road, while he was open-

ing the scriptures to us?' ... Then they told what had happened on the road, and how he had been made known to
them in the breaking of the bread. (Lk 24:32-35)

The offertory as a context for life's suffering
The offertory of the Mass provides a context within which we
can find the meaning and the value of our sufferings. In the offering of bread and wine that are to become the body and blood
of Jesus, we remember how he suffered throughout his life but
especially in his passion and death. Seen in this context we know
that we are not alone in our experience of suffering but that we
are accompanied by one who was familiar with all kinds of suffering and with the temptations these bring. (Heb 2:17-18, 4:14-
15)

The offertory is essentially a ritual in which we offer ourselves to God. Our basic offering is of our willingness to answer
Jesus' essential call to repent and to believe that God is loving
and provident. Suffering is the great challenge to this belief. It
questions our belief and in this way can either deepen it or damage it. Our willingness to wrestle with this challenge so that
life's dark side deepens our faith is an essential part of our offering at Mass. In the following prayer we reaffirm our belief that
the tragedies of sin cannot frustrate God's loving plans:

Almighty and ever-present Father,
your watchful care reaches from end to end
and orders all things in such power
that even the tensions and the tragedies of sin
cannot frustrate your loving plans.
(Opening prayer of week II)

Some suggestions for reflection and prayer
1. Read the following story and see what it says to you about
how growth filled suffering, may or may not be:

The Enemy Within
There was once a king who when he was defeated in battle

decided to devote the rest of his life to seeking God. So he set off with his wife and four sons on this quest. They were first confronted by the fire god, who asked the youngest son to part with his bow and arrows and trust in him. When he agreed, they travelled safely on through mountains and deserts and through the lands of hostile people. Their only real enemies now came from within. For example, the mother resented what the fire god had asked of her son and so she became weaker and weaker because of her bitter thoughts and she eventually died. The eldest son, thinking he knew better than the others, proudly went his own way. The next son spent all his energy trying to prove himself by removing a rock in the centre of the road which the others climbed over. The third son was a pleasure loving fellow who gave up when the journey became very difficult. The youngest son gave up because he was afraid when he no longer had his bow and arrows to defend himself. Only the father continued on in his search for God.

2. List some of the ways you suffer and then say a little about what for you is the most difficult one. Does this suffering take you in a positive or in a negative direction? Name a feeling you associate with suffering that is enlivening and one that is deadening.

3. Be in a quiet place with the side of you that has suffered and ask it about one of the ways it has suffered physically, emotionally, mentally or spiritually. In the conversation that ensues listen and respond to this often hidden side of yourself until you both have said all you want to. It is good to write down this conversation.

4. Reflect prayerfully on any of the following pieces of scripture in the light of what has emerged for you in 1-3 above: Jas 1:2-4, Job 42:1-6, Ps 23, Jn 16:20-33.

CHAPTER 12

The Art of Loving

In this chapter we examine how we learn to live consistently with the vision the Mass keeps before us and how we can do this most effectively by developing the most important art of all, the art of loving.

'The seed in your heart shall blossom'

John Quinn's suffering opened him up not only to himself and Olive but to others as well. His immersion in the loss of his wife made him more sensitive to and compassionate for those who had suffered a similar loss. After being through the sea of loss and having navigated its dangers, he was open to the person he met in St Stephen's Green who had his own tragedy to contend with. It was only after he had experienced the loss of everything, that the death of his wife initially appeared to be, that he could so graciously be with someone who had lost his good name and his livelihood. Even though he had never met this person before, he was capable of sharing with him what the death of Olive had meant to him. He was open also to this person's prophetic prediction when he uttered his mysterious parting words, 'The seed in your heart shall blossom.'

A sense of what is fair

Our sense of what is fair or just develops early in life. One of my most vivid memories of my time at a boarding school in the late forties is of meeting a boy who was in great pain after being punished. I was filled with anger for I felt he was being punished excessively and my heart went out to him. My memory of those times is that we never resented the severity of the punishment we received as long as it was fair. If we broke the rules we knew the price we had to pay. This was accepted provided everyone was treated in the same way and that the punishment met the crime. However, if boys we picked on or punished excessively we were indignant. I remember well the shock I experienced early on in my time at boarding school when the senior boys took the dramatic decision to go on strike because they felt they were being treated unfairly.

Doing the will of God

When I reflect back on these experiences now, I think we judged what was fair by our conscience or by whether it conformed or not to a sense of our own dignity that had developed at that stage of our lives. What made us indignant was when the inner authority of this voice within us, or our conscience, was not respected by an outer authority. During my years at school this outer authority was dominant and was associated with a body of rules we were expected to keep. The same was true when I went to the seminary where life was regulated by the rules which we were taught were the will of God for us.

Our prayer too was geared towards refining our sense of what God wanted us to do and towards motivating ourselves to do this. When we prayed we were encouraged to focus on the meaning and the message of a scene in the gospel we took for our prayer. The result was that every prayer period ended up in what might be called 'good advice' rather than 'good news'. For example, the meaning of the story of the Good Samaritan was that our love had to be practical and the message was that we needed to do more to give this concrete expression in the way we acted or behaved.

There was a concerted effort to change all this in Vatican II. It encouraged us to shift the emphasis from treating the gospels as a source of 'good advice' to renewing a sense of their being the good news Jesus proclaimed. (Mk 1:14-15) The emphasis shifted from seeing God's will as a revelation of what we are meant to do for God and others, to it being a revelation of God's loving plan. Thus God's will became a revelation of what God wants to do out of love for us, a revelation of a vision of ourselves as loved that would inspire all we do. In all of this there was a move away from being directed by an outer authority and to-wards being guided by the inner authority of our consciences or by the innate sense we all have from an early age of what is fair, just or right.

The law of consistency

When I was studying philosophy I had a love-hate relationship with a philosopher called Bernard Lonergan. I disliked the complexity of his writing and the imagery he used which was drawn largely from mathematics and science. On the other hand, many of the principles that underpin his philosophy have stayed with me and have served me well. For example, he writes about a *law of consistency* which is innate and says that the way we treat people must be consistent with the way we see them, with what we believe about them. This is the voice of our conscience which tells us when our behaviour is or is not consistent with the way we see others or with our vision of them.

The vision we come face to face with at Mass is of the over-whelming reality that we are loved 'to the utmost extent' and are thus utterly lovable. It follows from this that if we believe that we are this lovable, then others are so as well. If others have this extraordinary dignity that Jesus' love gives them, then certain ways of treating them are acceptable or fair and others are not. This is the reality that Jesus expresses in his commandment that we love others as he has loved us. What is involved in this com-mandment is more than an invitation that we imitate Jesus' way of relating with us. For example, the story of the Good Samaritan is more a picture of how practical Jesus' love is than a measure of how practical ours ought to be. The main thing this story asks us to do is to believe in Jesus' love, to accept that he is as loving and we as lovable as it portrays. If we accept this way of seeing ourselves, it has a profound influence on the way we see others, and nothing influences the way we treat people more than the way we see them. For example, if in Jesus' eyes we see ourselves as accepted in our weakness, this will do more for our acceptance of others in their weakness than any amount of advice we may get or give ourselves about tolerance or forgiveness.

The art of loving

Besides judging our behaviour as being or not being consistent with a vision we have of others, there is another way of evaluating the ways we relate. This is based on the belief that there is an art of loving which evaluates behaviour by the same standards that apply to any art. There is, in other words, a way of relating lovingly that is not only fair and just, not only true and good, but beautiful as well. If we think of beauty as something which is pleasing to the eye and which even arrests or captivates us, then we might ask ourselves, 'Are there people in our lives who relate in a way that catches our eye, arrests or captivates us and is thus truly beautiful?' As we look at Jesus' way of relating, is there a style about the way he relates that is captivating? Is there an art of loving, for example, in 'the gracious words that came from his mouth' (Lk 4:22) or in the gracious way he relates with the woman in Simon's house? (Luke 7:36-50)

A supernatural tact

Besides conscience, there is another capacity given to us as one of the seven Gifts of the Holy Spirit that is called Counsel. This gift empowers us to act with *a supernatural tact* so that we not only know what is *right* about the way we behave but what in addition is *just right*. Artists have a way of distinguishing what is just right from what is right or merely an adequate representation of what they wish to express. In pursuit of this they struggle with their material until it expresses what they want it to say in as perfect a way as is possible. So, I have written this chapter again and again in the hope that at some stage it will be just right, or at least as near to this ideal as is possible for me to get at this time.

The gift of Counsel enables us to develop what the psychologist, Erich Fromm calls 'the art of loving'. He believes that this is the greatest of all the arts but sadly the most neglected. In his book, *The Art of Loving*, he says that most people see love as 'a pleasant sentiment that happens as a matter of chance'. As a result, when people fall in love, they do not understand why it promises so much and yet seems to deliver so little. The reason for this disillusionment is that people fail to realise that love is an art. Like any other art, that of loving demands great skill and this is learned only with a great amount of disciplined effort. This is what is entailed in the lifelong struggle to develop this supernatural tact that allows us to discern, in all kinds of circumstances, what is 'the more excellent way' to love others. (1 Cor 12:31)

The aesthetics of relationship
The most important part of the Christian life, what Jesus calls 'the one thing necessary', is that we listen and respond to God's self revelation in Jesus, especially to the supreme moment of this revelation we have in the Mass. Finding ways to respond to this love in the style with which we relate is where we can be most creative in life. This is the main work of art which God commissions each of us with creating. We may be accustomed to think of aesthetics as a sensitivity to the beauty of what we call works of art, but there is a more important aesthetic which makes us sensitive to the beauty of the way we relate. We miss so much of the beauty life wants to reveal if we fail to notice and savour the beauty of the way others and we ourselves relate. We easily miss what Hopkins expressed so well when he wrote, 'For Christ plays in ten thousand places, lovely in limbs, and lovely in eyes not his.'

What is ultimately beautiful in life is to be found in the gospels, in the way, for example, Jesus is sensitive to and respects the Samaritan woman he met at the well. (Jn 4) We hear how impressed people were with 'the gracious way' he spoke. (Lk 4:22) His first disciples found the way he related with them so arresting that 'they left everything' just to be with him. (Lk 5:11) We see what James Joyce in his definition of beauty calls 'aesthetic arrest' in the way Jesus, when lifted up on the cross and at Mass, captivates people, drawing them to himself. (Jn 11:52, 12:19, 12:32)

Our guideline for developing the art of loving is Jesus' commandment that we love others as he has loved us. This commandment as we have seen is not primarily a call to imitate Jesus but to cultivate an eye for the style or artistry with which Jesus relates with us. By looking at Jesus in this way we gradually gain an intimate knowledge not only of how loving and lovable he is, but of how lovable we and others are in his eyes. If we believe in this love it provides us with a sense of security so that we become freer to go out to others in a way that is life-giving to ourselves and to them. Nothing deters us from going out to others in a healthy way more than a sense of our own insignificance or inadequacy. If we are not certain of and thus secure in the intensity of Jesus' love for us, of which Mass gives us a vision, we are inclined to seek a sense of significance and security elsewhere.

The creative power of affirmation

Even though the vision Jesus gives us at Mass of ourselves and others is the most important influence on the art of loving, it is also greatly influenced by our willingness to notice and affirm the style with which we and others relate. This is an important part of our mission to proclaim the good news or to notice, respect and appreciate a style of relating that is unique to each person. If we free ourselves from the tendency to focus on the deficiencies in the way we relate and focus instead on appreciating the skill with which we do it, this affirmation will do much more for us than any amount of advice we may give ourselves on how we might correct our deficiencies. We will thus become more aware of what is beautiful or stylish in the way we and others relate, more aware too of the gracious way we receive and return love within our relationships. In adverting to and owning the art of loving that we are already proficient at, we will be affirmed and encouraged to make the effort involved in this very creative side of our lives.

The Grace of God is in Courtesy

The last verse of Hilaire Belloc's poem, *Courtesy*, finds something God-like and beautiful in the art of loving:

Of Courtesy, it is much less
Than Courage of heart and Holiness,
But in my walks it seems to me
That the Grace of God is in Courtesy.

It is in appreciating the skill with which we and others relate that we make our holding environment real and engaging. In our effort to create and sustain this environment it is not so much a case of focusing on ways we can improve it as on becoming aware of how real and extensive it already is. We need to develop an eye for the beauty of this environment, for the sacrifices parents, for example, make to create and sustain it for their children.

The art of parenting

We take the work of parenting so much for granted that we do not realise how well so many people do what must be the most creative work in the world. Is it not after all the area of life where we are most generative and God-like? It is perhaps lack of appreciation of the creativity of parenting and the heroic nature of the sacrifices involved in it that has led to it being so undervalued as a full-time job, as our life's work. Yet, it is in these 'years and years of world without event' that God 'can crowd career with conquest'.

Yet God (that hews mountain and continent,
Earth, all, out; who, with trickling increment,
Veins violets and tall trees makes more and more)
Could crowd career with conquest while there went
Those years and years by of world without event
That in Majorca Alfonso watched the door.
(G. M. Hopkins)

Some suggestions for reflection and prayer

1. Read the following story a number of times and see what it says to you about how creative loving can be, about the art of loving.

> *Finding the Lion in the Stone*
> When the little boy asked the sculptor how he knew the magnificent lion he had carved was in the stone, he eventually got the answer, 'I had to find the lion in my heart first before I could find it in the stone!' The sculptor knew that even though he had to find it in his heart first, he would not have been happy to leave it there. He knew that it had to be given concrete expression and that what this produced had to be in harmony with what was in his heart. He had to wrestle with the stone until what he chiselled out of it was in keeping with what he had found in his heart.

2. Tell the story of the growth of the art of loving in your life. For example, you might recall one or two experiences when you became aware of the way you relate well or in a gracious or courteous way. Are there some people in your life who have influenced the way you relate or made you aware of how the 'Grace of God is in Courtesy'?

3. Enter into a fantasy about a celebration that is held in your honour. Your husband or wife, a close friend, someone who has worked alongside you, a former teacher and one of your children are asked to speak at the gathering. Note down the main thing each of these five say about you. Afterwards, in your inner room you listen to Jesus as he elaborates on what they have said and adds his praise of the way you relate to theirs.

4. Reflect prayerfully on how in Lk 19:1-10 Jesus *acknowledges* Zacchaeus' importance for him, *accepts his weakness, highlights his strengths* and is *concerned* for his welfare. Let Jesus highlight how loving you too are in these four ways.

PART 4

The transforming power of the Mass

In Part 4 we examine how abiding in Jesus' love in the way we reflected on in Part 3 can transform us. The magnetic power of his love can heal our wounds and set us free so that he can draw us into an intimate union with him.

Chapter 13 looks at how the magnetic attractiveness of the love Jesus reveals in the Mass can undo the divisive effects of sin and draw us into an intimate union with ourselves, with others and with all things.

Chapter 14 reflects on how the love Jesus reveals at Mass can heal the wounds that sin inflicts on us.

Chapter 15 examines how the attractiveness of the love Jesus reveals to us at Mass can free us from what separates us from him.

Chapter 16 focuses on how Jesus reconciles us to himself, or befriends all the areas of ourselves and others from which we have become estranged.

Lantana

The film *Lantana* takes it name from a shrub whose branches intertwine to form a very dense and complex undergrowth. This symbolises the tangled pattern of relationships the film focuses on. Central to these relationships is that of Leon and his wife Sonja. He is a detective whose life is complicated by an affair he is having with Joan, and this has a deadening effect on his relationship with Sonja his wife and with his two sons. She, in an effort to understand what has happened to their marriage, goes to Valerie, a psychiatrist whose own marriage to John is also a troubled one, as he is an academic who lives in his head and cannot respond to her emotionally.

Late one night on her way home, Valerie's car breaks down and she is picked up by Nick, the local mechanic. When he takes a short-cut she becomes suspicious and jumps out of the car. In her effort to escape she falls into a quarry and dies of her injuries. In investigating her disappearance Leon comes across a tape she made of a conversation she had with Sonja. From it Leon learns something about his wife which he finds hard to believe. This takes the form of three observations she has made to Valerie about her marriage. She says that what she misses most in it is a passionate relationship, one in which she is challenged to be emotionally honest. She also reveals that Leon's lack of emotional honesty is what troubles her most about the affair she knows her husband is having. However, when asked if she still loves her husband, she answers without any hesitation that she does.

The words of the tape, especially those about the steadfast nature of her love for him, have a deep influence on Leon and gradually bring about a profound change in him. This transformation begins to take shape when Joan, frustrated by Leon's unwillingness to leave his wife, decides to terminate her relationship with him. As a result, Leon realises for the first time how superficial their relationship has been. He also realises that his aggressive tendencies in his relationships and in his work lead him to the kind of injustice that, as a police officer, he is meant to be fighting against.

However, what affects Leon most deeply is the realisation that he has neglected the love of the one person who has stayed with him in spite of his tragic failure to respond to her love. As he listens to the way this love is expressed on the tape he becomes aware of his failure to respond to it. He gradually realises how close he has come to losing the love of the person who has been, and remains, the most constructive force in his life. When the tragedy of this dawns on him we have the film's most dramatic scene. Leon, a man hardened by his own selfishness and that of others, breaks down and weeps in a way that overwhelms his whole person and ours.

When he returns home he finds his wife sitting at the table, shocked into silence by what has happened to their marriage. All he can say as he sits down opposite her is, 'I don't want to lose you. I don't want to lose you.' She does not respond but sits in numbed silence. Wanting to leave her time to sit with what he has said to her, he goes to their bedroom and curls up on the bed like a wounded animal. She joins him and they lie side by side not looking at one another but perhaps at a vision of the tragedy of what might have been, and at a vision of the life of humbled love that might still be theirs.

The final scene of their reconciliation is of them dancing by themselves in the hall where they had gone to dancing classes. There he had seldom danced with her and when he had it was in a dispassionate way. Now they dance with a chastened passion as he gazes at her in a wholly absorbed way and she looks into the distance at a love she still believes is possible but it will take time for her to trust in again.

CHAPTER 13

'I will draw all to myself'

In Part 3 we saw how we can immerse ourselves in the love of Jesus which we examined in Part 2. In this chapter we focus on the transforming effect of this, on the profound effect the magnetic attractiveness of Jesus' love has on all our relationships. By drawing us to himself he draws us to each other and to all things.

Passionate fidelity

Most of the story told in the film *Lantana* is about the disintegrating effect on all Leon's relationships of his infidelity to his wife. As a result of his separation from her he finds himself at odds with his two sons and even with those with whom he works. There is an aggressiveness about the way he relates that drives a wedge between him and his fellow police officers and with those he deals with each day in the course of his work. The catalyst which changes all this, and effects a reintegration of all his relationships, is the tape he finds among the files of his wife's therapist. On it he is astounded to hear that his wife still loves him and despite his infidelity she still longs for a passionate relationship with him. What initially baffles him and eventually exhilarates him is that her love for him has survived his infidelity, his deceit and lack of emotional honesty that she has found so hard to bear.

The second call

When I was in my early fifties I came across an article entitled, *The Second Call*. It described three stages in the way most people answer the call to follow their dream before they are fifty. There is the enthusiasm of the first stage, the waning of this at the second and the finding of this enthusiasm again at the third.

However, the enthusiasm at this third stage differs greatly from that at the first stage in that it is experienced at a deeper and more enduring level.

I experienced the enthusiasm of the first stage when I decided to become a priest. I had moved away from any idea of this during my final years at school but shortly after I left school it suddenly struck me with overwhelming clarity that this was what I really wanted to do. My enthusiasm was whetted by a thirty day retreat I was brought through during my first month in the seminary. Even though I was ill-prepared for it, having had no training in the prayer and reflection it involved, it had a profound effect on me. I became involved in a relationship with Jesus that has remained the centre of my life ever since. But like all passionate relationships it has had its ups and downs, its peak and valley periods.

Doing too many good things
The second stage in the way I answered the call began about eight years after entering the seminary when I became intensely involved in the work I was doing as a teacher in a secondary school in Africa. It was my first taste of active work after the years of study so I relished the chance to share what I had learned in my studies. It was a time in my life of endless energy and intense activity. Though the contemplative side of me, represented by Mary, continued to have a say in my life, the more active Martha began to dominate. As well as teaching and getting engaged in a host of activities in the school where I taught, I filled in all the spare moments in my day writing text books and preparing them for publication.

It was only when I left my job as a secondary school teacher and began one in a teacher training college that I recognised how overactive I had become and how much the vision I had set out with had dimmed. Though I had not burnt myself out, I experienced the effects of withdrawal from so much activity in this much quieter time in my life. While it was not a depressing time, it was a dark one, as I felt isolated from the work I loved and the people I had come to know. As often happens, it was in this darkness that I heard a voice inviting me to begin my second journey. This was in answer to the 'second call' which invited me to enter the third stage of my journey. On this part of the journey I discovered again, in a quieter and more profound way, the enthusiasm I had known during my first months in the seminary.

When the centre no longer holds

What strikes me, as I reflect on these three stages, is how easy it is to drift out of the relationships that are central to life. This drifting can happen through neglect or through developing other interests that preoccupy us to the degree that the 'one thing necessary' becomes secondary. (Lk 10:38-42) Our tendency to drift is most damaging when it occurs in our relationship with God, for on this relationship all others depend. The book of Wisdom sees this tendency to drift as 'falling into deep forget-fulness' and its effect as the tragedy of 'getting cut of from God's kindness'. (Wis 16:11) Since it is God's kindness or care that makes and sustains us, losing touch with it leads to a disintegra-tion, not just of our relationship with God but of all our relation-ships. The image in Yeats' poem, *The Second Coming*, of things falling apart when the centre no longer holds, is very apt here.

Turning and turning in the widening gyre
The falcon cannot hear the falconer;
Things fall apart; the centre cannot hold;
Mere anarchy is loosed upon the world ...
The best lack all conviction, while the worst
Are full of passionate intensity.

Disintegration

In chapters 3-11 of the book of Genesis we have a profound de-piction of the nature of the anarchy that 'is loosed upon the world' when God is no longer the centre of our lives. All our re-lationships suffer as a result. When Adam and Eve excluded themselves from the garden, where everything centred on God, they were no longer at home with themselves. When they lost touch with God they lost touch with what was deepest about themselves. They became estranged from what was most God-like about them, the creative energy of their sexuality in its quest to become intimate and generative. Large areas of this energy became a source of temptation, seduction and shame. They felt they could no longer approach God so they hid. When asked why, Adam replied, 'I was afraid because I was naked, so I hid.' (Gen 3:10)

When Adam and Eve became estranged from God and thus from their inmost selves, they became estranged from each other. Adam blamed Eve and she blamed the serpent for what they should have assumed responsibility for themselves. We see how society disintegrates in the story of the tower of Babel, that ends the story of the Fall. Through building this tower people sought to reach a heaven of their own making. Their exclusion of God meant that the centre no longer held them together, they became scattered, cut off from themselves, from others and from their environment.

> Then they said, 'Come, let us build ourselves a city, and a tower with its top in the heavens, and let us make a name for ourselves; otherwise we shall be scattered abroad upon the face of the whole earth.' ... Therefore it was called Babel, because there the Lord confused the language of all the earth; and from there the Lord scattered them abroad over the face of all the earth. (Gen 11:4-9)

The disintegration which consumerism leads to
The divisive influence of separating ourselves from God, that the tower of Babel symbolises, is reproduced today in the divisive influence of our consumer culture. It has this influence as it focuses on our outer world, on 'getting and spending', on what we do and what we have. The dominance of our outer world that this leads to means that our inner world of relationships becomes secondary and is neglected. We no longer hear the call of adult life to go on a journey into the relationships that constitute our inner world.

The way our consumer culture erodes these relationships and so leads to their disintegration is strikingly described in the first chapter of John Kavanaugh's book, *Still Following Christ in a Consumer Society*. He explains how we have lost touch with our inner self as the demands of work leave us little time to explore this side of ourselves. When we lose touch with our inner self, intimacy, which consists in making known our inner self to others, becomes impossible. When in this way we become incapable of intimate relationships, we lose a sense of compassion and justice and so re-enact the Genesis story. We lose touch with ourselves and with others when we lose touch with God.

Jesus reintegrates all things

The gospels tell the story of how Jesus remedies this tragic situation by reintegrating all that has been disintegrated through sin. From the beginning of the gospel story we see Jesus drawing people to himself and becoming so attractive for them that they leave everything in order to be with him. (Lk 5:28) By the end of the gospel story Jesus has become so attractive that even the authorities who oppose him are forced to admit that the people as a whole are captivated by him, that 'the world has gone after him'. (Jn 12:19) This magnetic attractiveness of Jesus, that reintegrates all, reaches its climax in his passion, death and resurrection. When Jesus speaks about the influence of the love these events reveal in such a powerful way, he says that it will 'draw all people / all things' to him. (Jn 12:32) It will 'gather into one the dispersed children of God'. (Jn 11:52) This union we are drawn into is that which the Father, Jesus and the Spirit enjoy and want us to be part of.

> The glory that you have given me I have given them, so that they may be one, as we are one, I in them and you in me, that they may become completely one. (Jn 17:22-23)

Ultimately, what brings about this reintegration is the magnetic attractiveness of Jesus and especially of the greatest expression of his love that we expose ourselves to at Mass. (Jn 15:13) There

Jesus invites us to 'eat' and 'drink' or to 'abide in' this love as it is expressed in his body 'given up' for us and in his blood 'shed' for us.

> Take this, all of you, and eat it:
> this is my body which will be given up for you.

> Take this, all of you, and drink from it:
> this is the cup of my blood,
> the blood of the new and everlasting covenant.
> It will be shed for you and for all men
> so that sins may be forgiven.
> Do this in memory of me.

The unifying power of eating his body and drinking his blood is highlighted by Jesus when he says, 'Those who eat my flesh and drink my blood abide in me, and I in them. (Jn 6:56)

How Jesus works towards this union
In the early chapters of the gospels we have a description of the practical ways Jesus fosters this union into which he wishes to reintegrate everyone and everything. The most important way is that he makes space in his day to maintain his own union with his Father, and so we are told that 'In the morning, while it was still very dark, he got up and went out to a deserted place, and there he prayed.' (Mk 1:35) Jesus sees that he is sent by his Father 'to bring good news to the poor' and that this message of his Father's passionate love and all pervasive providence will heal people's blindness and set them free. (Lk 4:18)

Our desire to be reintegrated in Jesus so that we share in his own union with his Father is a major theme in the prayers of the Mass. For example, the communion prayers ask for 'the peace and unity of your kingdom'. Echoing the theme in John's gospel of Jesus' desire to gather into one family the dispersed children of God, we pray that we would be gathered together in being gathered to God. (Jn 11:52)

> From age to age you gather a people to yourself,
> so that from east to west

a perfect offering may be made
to the glory of your name.
(Eucharistic Prayer III)

He has come to lift up all things to himself,
to restore unity to creation.
(Preface of Christmas II)

In the prayers of the Mass we have specific ones for the different groups of people who are part of the union Jesus draws us into. For example we pray for the dead, for the church and to the saints in glory.

In union with the whole Church
we honour Mary,
the ever-virgin mother of Jesus Christ our Lord and God,
We honour Joseph, her husband,
the apostles and martyrs ... and all your saints.
(Eucharistic Prayer I)

In our longing for intimacy with Jesus, we pray that we might be free from our sins and from every evil so that we may never be parted from him.

Lord Jesus Christ, Son of the living God,
by the will of the Father and the work of the Holy Spirit
your death brought life to the world.
By your holy body and blood
free me from all my sins and from every evil.
Keep me faithful to your teaching
and never let me be parted from you. Amen
(Rite of Communion)

Some suggestions for reflection and prayer
1. Read the story of *Lantana* again and then ask yourself what strikes you most about the story.

2. Tell the story of a time when you lost a sense of the meaning of your life, a sense of purpose or of direction so that things fell apart for you and you felt scattered. How do you feel as you re-

call what happened, and what insight into what holds your life together did you get from the experience?

3. *The Tapestry Fantasy*

Be quiet for a while in your inner room and then let God join you. Imagine that there is a tapestry in the centre of the room that represents your life. God emphasises how beautiful it is in its design and range of colours. Not noticing any flaws in the tapestry, you ask where all the mistakes you made in life are to be found amid all this beauty. God smiles and says, 'I am the master tapestry maker and have made a feature out of these mistakes.' After pondering these words, tell God how you feel about them.

4. Reflect prayerfully on any of the following pieces of ccripture in the light of what you have experienced in 1-3 above: Jn 12:19, 12:32, 11:52, Eph 1:10 and Jn 21.

CHAPTER 14

The healing power of the Mass

In this chapter we examine how the wounds of the past need to be healed or they make the intimacy Jesus wants with us difficult to realise.

Healing power

When at the end of the film, *Lantana,* Leon returns to his wife he does so with a deep sense of failure. He has found himself rejected by Joan, the woman with whom he has been having an affair. He also faced the enormity of his betrayal of the one person who loved him faithfully and with a passion. As he curls up on his bed, after he has admitted his mistake to his wife and asked her forgiveness, he assumes the posture of a deeply wounded person. But in returning to his wife he knows that she is the one person who can heal him with the love he has discovered she still has for him.

When I was in my early twenties I failed an important exam. This meant that I had to repeat a whole year and since I was the only one of my group who had failed, I was on my own for that year in a limbo-like state. This was my first major experience of failure and its effect on my life was traumatic at the time as it resulted in a deep sense of shame and isolation. I had done my best and yet was found wanting. This experience has left a wound that will probably never be completely healed, as life's circumstances easily open this wound again, putting me in touch as they do with this sense of failure and loss of self esteem.

A basic wound we all share

The wound left by these early experiences of failure in our lives is only a small part of a much more serious wound that has two sources. One of these sources is our failure to live contentedly with our limitations and the other is our failure to face our sinfulness. For example, the wounds we pick up may be a sense of inadequacy due to our failure to measure up to our own expectations and to those of others. Our wounds may also be caused by things we do that damage our relationship with God and others.

The wounds may be inflicted by ourselves or by others. They are often due to a serious wrong we did and that we have never forgiven ourselves for, or they may be due to a wrong that was done to us and that we have never let go of so that it still haunts and saddens us. When we do not forgive ourselves or forgive others, the memories of our own sins and those of others can leave lasting wounds.

These wounds take the form of a vision of ourselves as inadequate and of the feelings this vision gives rise to. If we do not deal with this vision and the feelings it arouses this experience takes the form of a history of inadequacy that is inscribed in our hearts and minds. A lot of life's joy is eroded by the heart's feelings of frustration, guilt and sadness and more so by the mind's illusions of insignificance that our inadequacy feeds. We pay a great price for remaining unaware of how wounded our heart and mind is and of how much this debilitates us.

How the basic wound develops
To understand how the Mass can heal us it may help to examine how the wounds it seeks to heal usually develop.

- At first our wounds take the form of negative feelings like sadness that are debilitating because we fail to deal with them in a constructive way. As a result, these feelings persist and make us feel bad. It may be something we said in a moment of anger that causes us to judge that we made a fool of ourselves.

- Our wound becomes more serious when our negative feelings feed a poor self-image. This false image emerges when we allow a small area of our lives, where we fail to live up to a standard we have set for ourselves, to colour the picture we have of ourselves. It may be that we judge ourselves a failure because we have not performed well in a small area of our life, say in 10% of it. The other 90% may be admirable but what is negative tends to hold our attention and dominate our view of ourselves.

- Thirdly, our poor self-image can erode or even block our belief. When this happens, we do not live with the image of ourselves we see reflected back to us in the eyes of Jesus when he says that he loves us just as the Father loves him. We find this reality, and the language Jesus uses to express it, unrealistic because it challenges us to believe that we have a significance we cannot accept or believe in.

A wound that affects mind and heart

The basic wound we live with springs from the mind's illusions and from the heart's debilitating feelings. These feelings such as sadness, guilt or fear, especially when they become habitual, are the source of much of our physical, mental and spiritual illnesses. Though these debilitating feelings are the more obvious signs of our woundedness, they have their roots in the way we see ourselves, in a distorted image of ourselves. This gainsays the image Jesus wants us to believe in. This is the image we are given at Mass, of ourselves as loved 'to the utmost extent', as loved by Jesus as he is by his Father.

As the Father has loved me, so I have loved you; abide in my love. (Jn 15:9)

If we believe what Jesus says here, it changes the way we see ourselves so that we come to realise we are immensely significant. This change of mind effects a change of heart in that it leads to a joy that Jesus says is a share in his own.

I have said these things to you so that my joy may be in you, and that your joy may be complete. (Jn 15:11)

The worth we earn is inadequate

Seeing ourselves as significant and the joy this leads to is so important for us that if we do not accept it as God's gift we will go all out to earn it. We are tempted, like Jesus was, to earn our significance through our own efforts. (Lk 4:1-13) However, because we are made for the significance that God's gift of love gives us, what we attain by our own efforts is always inadequate. This is because human love, and the sense of significance it gives us, is fragile, fleeting and superficial. The deficiency of the love we have earned by our own efforts is so much part of us that getting rid of it is like getting rid of the seven evil spirits that Jesus says have taken up residence within us. They are impossible to dislodge by our own efforts.

> When the unclean spirit has gone out of a person, it wanders through waterless regions looking for a resting place, but it finds none. Then it says, 'I will return to my house from which I came.' When it comes, it finds it empty, swept, and put in order. Then it goes and brings along seven other spirits more evil than itself, and they enter and live there. (Mt 12:43-45)

How the Mass heals us

Rather than trying to earn our own worth and to heal by our own efforts the wound our sense of insignificance inflicts on us, Jesus proposes another way. This is that we would accept the immense significance that he wants to give us as part of what he calls, 'the gift of God'. (Jn 4:10) This gift is of a vision of our true worth that the Mass keeps before us, a vision revealed to us in the powerful way the Mass states that we are loved passionately, profoundly and in an everlasting way. If we learn to believe that we are loved in this way and are thus this lovable, our lives take on the utmost significance. It is our faith in this reality that heals us more than anything else.

> 'Daughter, your faith has made you well; go in peace, and be healed of your disease.' (Mk 5:34)

The faith that Jesus speaks about here is an intimate knowledge of being loved in a way that knows no limitation. If in the Mass we are given a vision of ourselves as loved 'to the utmost extent', does it not follow that we are utterly lovable and of the utmost significance in the eyes of Jesus? The full impact of this love is not addressed to us just as a group but as individuals. Each of us is faced with the overwhelming reality that Paul was faced with when he admitted, Jesus 'loved me and gave himself for me'. (Gal 2:20)

The healing miracles
We can see how Jesus nurtured this faith that heals us in the healing miracles he worked. The importance of these miracles to Jesus' plan to draw us into an intimate relationship with him can be judged from the amount of time he spent healing people in the gospels. Through these miracles Jesus seeks to nurture the faith that is the source of inner healing. So, the more obvious outer healing is a sign of an inner healing brought about by faith in the love and providence of God that the miracles reveal. In this way, the miracles Jesus works are similar to the wonderful works that God performed out of love for the Israelites during the Exodus. From all these wonderful works that God worked during the 40 years of the Exodus, Moses came to the following conclusion about the nature of God's love and providence:

> The Lord passed before him, and proclaimed, 'The Lord, the Lord, a God merciful and gracious, slow to anger, and abounding in steadfast love and faithfulness, keeping steadfast love for the thousandth generation, forgiving iniquity and transgression and sin. (Ex 34:6-7)

In John's gospel seven of these wonderful works or signs are focused on to bring out different aspects of the last and greatest of them. This is the death and the resurrection of Jesus and it is seen by Jesus to be the most powerful expression of his love.

> No one has greater love than this, to lay down one's life for one's friends. (Jn 15:13)

A healing vision and a way of absorbing it

As well as providing the vision of Jesus' love that heals us, the Mass gives us a way of absorbing this love or of believing in it. This is what Jesus means when he invites us to 'eat' his body given up for us and to 'drink' his blood poured out for us.

In one of the prayers of the Mass we express our belief that 'eating', or savouring and assimilating the love of Jesus, brings 'health of mind and body'.

> Lord Jesus Christ,
> with faith in your love and mercy
> I eat your body and drink your blood,
> Let it not bring me condemnation ,
> but health of mind and body.
> *(Celebrant's private preparation)*

Many of the prayers of the Mass, such as the following one, are an expression of our belief in Jesus' desire to heal us.

> Lord, I am not worthy to receive you,
> but only say the word and I shall be healed.
> *(Rite of Communion)*

In a prayer of St Thomas Aquinas for after communion, the healing power of the Mass is appealed to a number of times:

> I who am sick approach the physician of life.
> I who am unclean come to the fountain of mercy;
> blind, to the light of eternal brightness,
> poor and needy, to the Lord of heaven and earth.
> Therefore, I implore you in your boundless mercy
> to heal my sickness, cleanse my defilement,
> enlighten my blindness, enrich my poverty,
> and clothe my nakedness.
> Then shall I dare to receive the bread of angels,
> the King of kings and Lord of lords,
> with reverence and humility,
> contrition and love.

Some suggestions for reflection and prayer

1. Reflect on the following story and see what it says to you about feelings like resentment that you carry around with you.

> Two monks on a long journey were walking through the muddy streets of a town when one of them noticed a beautifully dressed woman trying to cross the street. He took her in his arms and put her down where she wanted to go. Later he noticed his companion was very silent so he asked if anything was the matter. When his companion rebuked him for what he had done he replied, 'I let go of her when I put her down, but you have been holding onto her ever since.'

2. Recall an experience which has left you wounded. Is this wound healed wholly or partially or is it still raw and easy for similar experiences to open again? Is there something you can do to heal this wound?

3. Enter a dialogue with the wounded side of yourself by writing down one or two things you want to say to it and then write down what this wounded self says in reply.

4. Reflect prayerfully on the woundedness of the two disciples Jesus joins on the road to Emmaus. (Lk 24:13-24) Notice how Jesus goes about healing them mentally and emotionally so that rather than seeing life in a way that causes feelings of sadness, they are filled with hope and joy. You may also like to reflect on Mk 1:40-42 and Lk 8:48 in the light of your experience of what happened on the road to Emmaus.

CHAPTER 15

To set captives free

Freedom, as well as healing, is necessary if Jesus is to draw us into an intimate relationship with him. In this chapter we will see how the attractiveness of Jesus' love can free us from what separates us from him, from the divisive effects of sin.

Love that sets free

For much of the film, *Lantana*, Leon is seeking happiness in the wrong places. He is seduced by the pleasure of his affair with Joan and by his aggressive desire to be in control in every situation he is in. This leaves him listless or with little energy for his relationships with his wife and two sons. It is only at the end of the film when he has learned to value his relationship with his wife more than anything else that we feel he is free again. This is because she has won back his heart and set him free from the dominance of trivial and fleeting attractions. In realising how intense, profound and enduring is the love of his wife for him, Leon sees that, in relation to this love, all others are secondary. At the end of the film we are in no doubt that there is only one love that matters, only one he knows he cannot afford to lose. This realisation sets him free.

Finding love's liberty

I left school in 1953 with no clear idea about what I wanted to do. I had a vague idea of studying engineering as I was interested in technology, such as it was then. During my final few years at school I had distanced myself from the idea of becoming a priest as my interests lay elsewhere. I loved all kinds of sport, I was passionate about radio and films and I read a lot of novels.

However, mid-way through the summer holidays of the year I left school, I suddenly felt drawn to give the idea of becoming a priest a final consideration. When I read a pamphlet by Fr Willie Doyle on the idea of a vocation to the priesthood, I became convinced that this was what I really wanted to do.

There were plenty of things that militated against my choosing to devote myself to this 'unreal' world of the priesthood. It was not that the world of the priest was disdained, as it is by many today, but it was a world apart from that of most of my family and friends. What liberated me from the fear of taking this road less travelled was the experience of coming to know Jesus and how attractive he quickly became for me. Apart from the influence of my parents' faith, what brought about this conversion was my experience of the *Spiritual Exercises of St Ignatius* which we did during our first month in the seminary. Even though I was ill-prepared for this experience it had a profound effect on me. It was only many years later that I saw how free this experience left me, how liberated I was by it.

When I look back on what was happening to me then, I realise that it was in many ways similar to what was happening to my brothers and sisters as each in turn fell in love and got married. Before they fell in love they were possessed by the normal demons of adolescence. They were touchy, mercurial in their moods and clung to their own space and possessions. When they fell in love, however, their beloved seemed to have the power to liberate them from their demons so that they became new people. I began to enjoy their company and regretted that they were not around as much as they were before they fell in love.

Something similar had happened to me, though I did not see the similarity at the time. As I came to know Jesus, I came under his spell so that in a real sense I became a free man, as the importance of everything became relative to the importance of being with him. I became free from many of the things that had dominated my attention before Jesus enthralled me. Since noticing the unusual kind of falling in love that has occurred in my life, John Donne's lines about this experience enchant me every time I read them:

> Except you enthral mee, never shall be free,
> Nor ever chaste, except you ravish mee.

A gospel of liberation

Setting people free from the demons that enslaved them, so that they would be free to be with him in an intimate way, was central to what Jesus came to do. Luke hears Jesus saying at the beginning of his public life that he has come 'to proclaim release to the captives' and 'to let the oppressed go free'.

> The Spirit of the Lord is upon me, because he has anointed me to bring good news to the poor. He has sent me to proclaim release to the captives and recovery of sight to the blind, to let the oppressed go free. (Lk 4:18)

In the Mass we address Jesus as the 'Lamb of God' who takes away the sins of the world, or as the one who liberates us from the enslaving power of sin. To understand this image of Jesus as our liberator we need to look at its origins in the book of Exodus. There we see that it was the blood of the lamb, smeared on the doorposts of the houses of the Israelites, that liberated them. Freed from slavery in Egypt, they were free to set out on their journey to the Promised Land. On this journey it gradually became clear that the real slavery was not imposed on them from the outside. It was an internal one they subjected themselves to when they sinned.

Gradually the Israelites realised that what set them free from their enslavement to sin was the attractiveness of God's love that they discovered in the Exodus experience. However, the ultimate proof of this love is revealed at Mass when Jesus, as the lamb of God, sheds his blood for us. It is when this love is allowed to exercise its full attractiveness on us that it sets us free from anything that would separate us from it. In other words, when we get an intimate knowledge of this love it draws us to Jesus so powerfully that it makes the attractiveness of all else seem relatively unimportant. (Jn 12:32) In the following prayers from the Mass Jesus is depicted as the lamb of God who sets us *free from* what enslaves us as well as *free to* enjoy his peace or all 'his supper' symbolises:

Lamb of God who takes away the sins of the world,
grant us peace.
(Rite of Communion)

Casting out demons

We see the external form of this liberation in the gospels when Jesus 'casts out demons'. This is one of the main works that Jesus devotes himself to and it is a sign of his desire to free us from what dominates or enslaves us. We have a dramatic example of Jesus setting a person free from the demons that dominated him in the case of Legion.

They came to Jesus and saw the demoniac sitting there, clothed and in his right mind, the very man who had the legion ... As he was getting into the boat, the man who had been possessed by demons begged him that he might be with him. But Jesus refused, and said to him, 'Go home to your friends, and tell them how much the Lord has done for you, and what mercy he has shown you.' And he went away and began to proclaim in the Decapolis how much Jesus had done for him; and everyone was amazed. (Mk 5:15-20)

Liberation is a lifetime's work

Those in the gospels who, like Legion, have demons cast out of them, symbolise a profound need we all have to be set free from what oppresses us. Even though the way we are dominated by evil spirits is much less obvious than in the case of Legion, it is as real and restricting. Our liberation differs from that of Legion also in that it takes place over a long period, where that of Legion seems to have been instantaneous. Liberation for us is the fruit of a lifetime of disciplined effort.

One of the reasons why it takes us so long to attain the freedom Jesus offers us is that we do not recognise that our demons are more internal than external. Our demons take the form of negative feelings such as anger, fear or sadness and the illusions that generate these feelings. If we allow these illusions and feelings to become habitual they enslave us, we become 'the slaves of the one whom we obey'.

> Do you not know that if you present yourselves to anyone as obedient slaves, you are slaves of the one whom you obey, either of sin, which leads to death, or of obedience, which leads to righteousness? (Rom 6:16)

In this passage from Paul's letter to the Romans he sees two influences at work on us, both bidding for our allegiance. We, like Rapunzel, have to choose who we 'obey' or listen to and then accept the consequences of our choice.

Who do you listen to?
There was once a young girl called Rapunzel who was very beautiful. She came under the influence of a witch, who knew that if she wanted to hold on to her she had to convince her that she was ugly. The witch feared that if Rapunzel realised she was beautiful, she would go off with one of the young men who came to consult the witch. If on the other hand, she was convinced she was ugly, she would be afraid of being seen by them, and would therefore hide when they were around. So the witch gradually convinced Rapunzel that she was ugly and when anyone came to the witch's house Rapunzel hid for fear of being seen.

One day when Rapunzel was in her room combing her hair, she became conscious of someone looking at her through the window behind her. Instinctively she turned around and in the eyes of the young man gazing at her through the window she saw that she was beautiful. Gradually, as she learned to believe this, her fear was replaced by joy. Eventually, she set off on the long journey of freeing herself from the deadening influence of the witch in order to accept the life and happiness which the young man's love opened up before her.

The two ways
Like Rapunzel we can choose to believe the significant people in

our lives who, similar to the young man in the story, reflect back to us a healthy image of ourselves. Chief among these significant people for the Christian are the three persons of the Trinity. What we see in their eyes is 'the good news' of their love and our lovableness. This is 'the good news' they ask us to believe in. If we do choose to believe in this it will generate a range of good feelings, chief among which is the complete joy Jesus promises will be ours if we abide in his love.

As the Father has loved me, so I have loved you; abide in my
love ... I have said these things to you so that my joy may be
in you, and that your joy may be complete. (Jn 15:9-11)

The other option the Rapunzel story puts before us is that we choose to believe those whom the witch symbolises. They tempt us to believe that life is all about pleasure, power or sloth. These are the three things Jesus was tempted to put at the centre of his life. (Lk 4:1-13) The temptation to centre our lives on pleasure is one our consumer culture promotes. It invites us to believe that the good life is the pleasant one and urges us to avoid what is unpleasant and the onerous effort that a lasting joy requires. Then there is the temptation to seek the power that wealth and success offer us. We succumb to this temptation when we make what we possess and the work we do to possess it our priority in life. Perhaps the most subtle of the temptations is to sloth. This temptation is to be lazy or to avoid taking responsibility for the taxing task of making our inner world of relationships our primary concern.

Becoming enslaved, imprisoned or confined

In as far as we give into any of these temptations our lives become confined. 'We become the slaves of what we obey' (Rom 6:16) when we put at the centre of our lives anything other than the unlimited love of God we are made for. If we do make anything other than this love the centre of our lives, it imprisons us within the limitations of what it can offer us. We become imprisoned within the confines of the barnyard rather than having the sky for our limit.

Having the sky for your limit

There was once a poultry farmer who was given a present of an eagle's egg. He decided to experiment by putting it with some eggs a hen was hatching out. In due course the eagle emerged with the chicks and grew up with them in the very confined area of the barnyard. Even though it was never quite the same as the chickens, it adapted itself to their ways and it always thought of itself as one of them and acted as such. One day when it was about a year old, its eye was caught by the inspiring sight of an eagle in full flight. This caused something to stir within the young eagle. However, it was soon brought back to earth by a cock telling it to stop star-gazing and to get on with the job.

Now, there are two endings to the story. One has the young eagle putting its head back down as it had been told and continuing for the rest of its days within the very limited world of the barnyard. The other ending is that, inspired by the vision in the sky, the young eagle stretched its wings and took off into the sky. Never again was it confined to the barnyard as from then on it had the sky for its limit.

We confine ourselves to a corner of life when we move God from the centre of it and put pleasure, success or sloth there instead. By contrast, Jesus wants us to have the sky for our limit, to enter into and enjoy the unlimited life he offers.

I came that they may have life, and have it abundantly. (Jn 10:10)

Jesus himself *is* this life, this abundance, this banquet and he comes to each person's door seeking to share it.

Listen! I am standing at the door, knocking; if you hear my voice and open the door, I will come in to you and eat with you, and you with me. (Rev 3:20)

The tragedy of our refusal to partake in the abundance of life which Jesus wants us to enjoy is illustrated by the foolishness of the guests who refuse to come to the banquet. Something else is more important for them.

Then Jesus said to him, 'Someone gave a great dinner and invited many. At the time for the dinner he sent his slave to say to those who had been invited, "Come; for everything is ready now." But they all alike began to make excuses. The first said to him, "I have bought a piece of land, and I must go out and see it; please accept my regrets." Another said, "I have bought five yoke of oxen, and I am going to try them out; please accept my regrets." Another said, "I have just been married, and therefore I cannot come." (Lk 14:16-20)

Setting captives free
Jesus' way of setting us free, so that we can come to the feast he has prepared for us in the Mass, is through winning us over by his attractiveness. We realise how powerful this attractiveness is for his first disciples when we see them 'leaving everything in order to be with him'. (Lk 5:11) He must have had an extraordinary appeal for these people, who had been fishermen all their lives, to lead them to leave the security of this for the precarious existence of following an itinerant preacher.

As the gospel story unfolds, the drawing power of Jesus' love, the revelation of its length and breadth and height and depth, has its effect. We see this in the early stages of the gospel story when Jesus worked a miracle to save a family the embarrassment of running out of wine at their wedding feast. (Jn 2:1-11) In this act of kindness the disciples 'saw his glory', or the radiance of his love. They were so won over by how authentic and beautiful his love was that they believed in him. The gradual revelation of this love and its 'glory' or beauty, leads Jesus' disciples, at a critical point in John's gospel, to say that there is nothing in life that they want more than to be with him.

Because of this many of his disciples turned back and no longer went about with him. So Jesus asked the twelve, 'Do you also wish to go away?' Simon Peter answered him, 'Lord, to whom can we go? You have the words of eternal life. We have come to believe and know that you are the Holy One of God.' (Jn 6:66-69)

'The truth shall set you free'

The glory of Jesus, or the radiance of his love, and his disciples' faith in it, is severely tested when he begins to tell them about his passion and death. However, it is clear from the way they continue to follow him, and even pledge themselves to die with him, that Jesus has won them over completely. He has become so important for them that the value of everything else is relative to being with him. By the way he has enthralled them, he has loosened the grip on them of all else in their lives. In this context we see what Jesus means when he says, 'The truth shall make you free.' The word 'truth' here means that Jesus is the love of his Father made visible, that he is the full extent, depth and intensity of this love expressed in human terms. Thus, the truth sets us free in the sense that his love becomes so attractive that nothing can compete with it. This is the awesome reality expressed in the parable of the pearl and the hidden treasure. We catch a glimpse of this reality when something we wish to attain becomes so much a priority that all else becomes relatively unimportant. We become free to pursue the one thing we want, we sell all else to attain it.

> The kingdom of heaven is like treasure hidden in a field, which someone found and hid; then in his joy he goes and sells all that he has and buys that field. Again, the kingdom of heaven is like a merchant in search of fine pearls; on finding one pearl of great value, he went and sold all that he had and bought it. (Mt 13:44-46)

When Jesus is 'lifted up' on the cross and gives us the greatest sign of his love, his attractiveness becomes truly magnetic. (Jn 12:32) By constantly renewing our awareness of the intensity of his love for each of us, as we do at Mass, we grow in freedom and are less likely to be enslaved by anything else. We are gradually released from the bonds that bind us. This does not mean that we value anything less but that compared to the love of Jesus all else becomes relative. For Paul, the hold of everything on him is as nothing compared to the hold of the love of Jesus.

More than that, I regard everything as loss because of the surpassing value of knowing Christ Jesus my Lord. For his sake
I have suffered the loss of all things, and I regard them as
rubbish, in order that I may gain Christ and be found in him,
not having a righteousness of my own that comes from the
law, but one that comes through faith in Christ, the righteousness from God based on faith. (Phil 3:8-9)

Mass as a key to freedom

We will conclude this chapter with a sampling of the ways our
desire for freedom and Jesus' wish to satisfy this desire is expressed in the Mass. In the following extract from the 4th
Eucharistic Prayer Jesus is seen as the one the Father sends to
proclaim 'to prisoners, freedom'.

To the poor he proclaimed the good news of salvation,

to prisoners, freedom,

and to those in sorrow, joy.

In the following memorial acclamation it is stated that it is in the
death and resurrection that we find true freedom.

Lord, by your cross and resurrection

you have set us free.

You are the Saviour of the world.

In other prayers of the Mass, Jesus is addressed as the Lamb of
God who takes away the sins of the world. He thus delivers us
from the worst form of slavery.

Some suggestions for reflection and prayer

1. Read again the story above about the eagle's egg. What tends
to confine *you* within the limits of the barnyard?

2. Tell the story of a time in your life when you became over-in-
volved in something like work, pleasure, success, or a relationship so that you lost your freedom. If you have managed to free
yourself from this excessive involvement, say how you did so.

3. After you have quietened yourself in a place where you like to

be alone, let Jesus join you. He asks you about what confines you to a corner of life and prevents you from having the sky for your limit. He talks to you about how you might gain your freedom.

4. Reflect prayerfully on any of the following pieces of scripture in the light of what has emerged for you in 1-3 above: Mk 5:1-20, Rom 6:16, Lk 4:18, Phil 3:8-9.

CHAPTER 16

Reconciliation

In chapters 14 and 15 we have seen how Jesus heals us and sets us free so that we may enter an intimate relationship with him. In this chapter we look at how Jesus reconciles us with ourselves, others and all things, drawing all the areas of our life from which we have become estranged into an intimate relationship with him.

The need of acceptance
In the course of the film, *Lantana,* Leon undergoes a profound change. At the beginning of the film he is unfaithful to his wife and makes little effort to relate with his colleagues. He is badly in need of a more reconciliatory attitude to those around him. The one person who can bring about this change of attitude is Sonya his wife as she still loves him in a deep and enduring way. By the end of the film the attractiveness of her love for him has again asserted its hold on him. He now seeks to be reconciled to her on her terms and at her pace. This is wonderfully expressed by how attentive and accommodating he is to her as they dance together in the closing scene of the film.

Becoming estranged from areas of life
It is 50 years since I decided to become a priest. Answering this call involved taking 'a road less travelled' so that I gradually lost touch with many areas of life most people are at home in. The communities I lived in, especially in my early years, were exclusively male and so I got cut off from the world of women, from marriage, from having a family of my own and from much of what is part of the way most people live. During the 17 years I

was a missionary, I lived on the fringe of a culture in which I was largely a stranger. I was not able to communicate easily with the people I lived among and thus not able to come to know them well or make friends among them.

However, in spite of the unusual nature of the road I was invited to take, it has led me to so many good things that I would not have its winding ways otherwise, even if I were given the chance to arrange what has happened differently. But it has meant that for 20 or so years after I left school I got cut off and even estranged from large areas of life. Only in my 40s did I begin to realise this and much later still to understand the importance of reconciliation as a way of befriending all those areas of life from which I had become estranged. It is in this context that the Sacrament of Reconciliation has begun to take on a new meaning for me. In practice, it has involved becoming aware of what I had become estranged from, how impoverishing this was and how I could befriend those areas of life from which I had become estranged.

Our tendency to limit our horizons
A reason why we become estranged from certain areas of life is that we have a tendency to divide the world into 'them' and 'us', into those who are strangers and those we are familiar with. We learn early in life that there are areas of our environment that are hostile. This encourages a wariness about many areas of experience and gradually limits the scope of our sensitivity and compassion to a circle of people and things with which we are familiar and comfortable. This leads to a lack of sensitivity to and concern for those outside this circle and can lead to a neglect of and an indifference to them.

The scope of our sensitivity and compassion is further limited by our prejudices. For example, our world is divided into the haves and the have-nots as we tend to divide the world according to what people do and how much they have, so that the unemployed and the poor may not be a prime concern. Again, we tend to identify with either the world of men or of women and get cut off or estranged from the masculine or feminine side of ourselves and others. We also tend to divide our world into an outer and an inner one. Due to the influence of our consumer culture's emphasis on our outer world, our inner one may have become unfamiliar, unimportant and even foreign.

We become estranged from other areas of life due to neglect. For example, we may be unaware of the significant people in our story and of how their love has made and sustained us. If we are out of touch with people like our parents and all they have told us about ourselves in the various ways they have loved us, we are out of touch with our deeper selves. When we are estranged from our inmost self we become incapable of much of the intimacy we long for, which is by definition a making known this inmost self. This loss of identity and our capacity for intimacy often leads to a lack of sensitivity, compassion and justice.

The call to expand our horizons

In the last few chapters we have been looking at how the growing attractiveness of Jesus, especially as presented to us at Mass, can transform us. If we give his magnetism a chance to work its way with us, it can reintegrate and reorder out lives. However, we have seen that if by his attractiveness Jesus is to *draw us to himself* it is necessary that he *heals* the wound of our insignificance and *sets us free* from what separates us from him. Once this union with Jesus has been restored, we are in a position to draw into it areas of ourselves and others we have become estranged from. This befriending of those areas of life we have become separated from is what we mean by reconciliation. It is into this reconciliation that Jesus seeks to guide us through his commandment that we love others as he has loved us. (Jn 15:12)

The calls of adult life

A way of understanding this call of Jesus to be reconciled with him, with ourselves and with others is to see it in terms of answering *the four calls of adult life*. These four were worked out by the psychoanalyst Erik Erikson as part of what he saw as the adult life cycle. They are the calls to *identity, intimacy, generativity and integrity.*

By revealing the good news of his love for us, Jesus reveals our true *identity,* or who we are for him. If we become aware of our true identity by reflecting on the events of our story, and articulate for ourselves the insights into ourselves which this stimulates, we can then make these known to others. In this way we answer the second call of adult life, the call to *intimacy.* When Jesus befriends us he calls us into a profound level of intimacy. He wants to make known to us 'everything' about the most profound relationship of his life, that with his Father.

> I do not call you servants any longer, because the servant does not know what the master is doing; but I have called you friends, because I have made known to you everything that I have heard from my Father. (Jn 15:15)

This degree of intimacy that Jesus calls friendship is possible with only a small number of people. However, if we form this kind of relationship with a few people it provides an environment into which we can draw others. Thus by answering the first two calls to identity and intimacy we are enabled to answer the third. This is the call to become *generative* or to become more and more inclusive in the way we relate. The fourth call, to *integrity,* is one associated mainly with the latter years of our life. It is a call to reflect on and to share with our friends and our family, with our children and our grandchildren, a wisdom we have learned from answering the first three calls. This is a wisdom about life as Jesus saw it, a wisdom learned from a lifetime's experience of keeping the great commandment. This is a huge body of experience we have of the love we have received and returned within the main relationships we have been involved in throughout life.

> Just then a lawyer stood up to test Jesus. 'Teacher,' he said, 'what must I do to inherit eternal life?' He said to him, 'What is written in the law? What do you read there?' He answered, 'You shall love the Lord your God with all your heart, and

with all your soul, and with all your strength, and with all your mind; and your neighbour as yourself.' And he said to him, 'You have given the right answer; do this, and you will live.' (Luke 10:25-28)

How we befriend all we are estranged from

Jesus' call to reconciliation, or to befriend all the areas of our lives we have become estranged from, is based on what he calls his commandment that we love others as he has loved us. (Jn 15:12) Keeping this commandment involves developing a number of important abilities by which we befriend others. There is first of all the ability to *acknowledge* others and this involves becoming sensitive to and respecting their dignity. Then there is the ability to befriend others by *accepting* their limitations and waywardness in order that we may *appreciate* their strengths or gifts. Finally, befriending others involves being *concerned for* their welfare.

We see how Jesus befriends Zacchaeus in the way he *acknowledges* him. In a symbolic gesture Jesus invites him in from the periphery of the crowd to become the centre of attention. Even though the crowd is hostile to Zacchaeus, and he himself admits they have a reason to be so, Jesus *accepts* him and demonstrates this by arranging to have a meal with him. Jesus also *appreciates* Zacchaeus' dignity, insisting that he is as much a son of Abraham as any of those standing around. The fact that Jesus is willing to incur the displeasure of the crowd and to spend time with and make much of Zacchaeus is a sign of how *concerned* he is for his welfare. (Lk 19:1-10)

The Sacrament of Reconciliation

What often proves to be the biggest obstacle to reconciliation is the non-acceptance of our own limitations and sinfulness. We get fixated with these and with the frustration, guilt and sadness they often give rise to. However, if we do not befriend this poor side of ourselves, by accepting it, we will not be able to appreciate and believe in how loved and lovable we really are in Jesus' eyes. If this happens, the good news of God's love and our lovableness, that Jesus spends his life teaching us to believe in, will always appear too good to be true. It will be too far beyond our estimation of ourselves to be realistic. To befriend this weak and wayward side of ourselves is the key to developing all our relationships. In this context it becomes easier for us to understand the basic reason why Jesus gave us the *Sacrament of Reconciliation*. He meant it to teach us how to accept our poverty or the limited and sinful side of ourselves. If we do accept our poverty, we will then be disposed to forgive and accept the sinful side of others so that it does not block our appreciation of them. (Mt 9:5-6)

Reconciliation and forgiveness

Our difficulty of understanding and appreciating the Sacrament of Reconciliation may arise from a faulty understanding of forgiveness. We may associate forgiveness with forgetting or putting aside the hurt we feel when others wrong us. However, the fact is that we do not have this kind of control over our feelings that we can put them aside at will. What we do control is the main element in forgiveness which is our acceptance of the limitations and sinfulness of others. But for this to be effective we have first of all to grow in acceptance of our own limitations and weaknesses. For example, if we learn to see our sinfulness in the accepting way Jesus sees the sinfulness of Zacchaeus, it is most likely that we will be more accepting of the weaknesses of others.

Levels of forgiveness and acceptance

There are four levels of this acceptance that Jesus seeks to lead us into. At the first level Jesus asks us to accept his forgiveness or the fact that he is content to walk with this limited and sinful side of us. Knowing how difficult it is for us to overcome our poor self-image, and how important it is that we do, Jesus gives us the Sacrament of Reconciliation or what is in a sense a sacrament of self-acceptance. If the sacrament helps us to accept Jesus' acceptance of us, this will do more for our acceptance of the limitations and sinfulness of others than any amount of advice we may give ourselves about how we should feel about and treat this shadow side of them. Through cultivating this acceptance we will live more contentedly with what is symbolised by the weeds amid the wheat.

> The slaves said to him, 'Then do you want us to go and gather them?' But he replied, 'No; for in gathering the weeds you would uproot the wheat along with them. Let both of them grow together until the harvest.' (Mt 13:28-30)

We find a second level of Jesus' acceptance of our weakness expressed in the letter to the Hebrews. There it says that Jesus is able to 'sympathise with our weakness' since through his incarnation he has first-hand knowledge of our limitations. He also knows our temptations from the inside, since 'in every respect he has been tested as we are'. He is not on a pedestal above the human condition but in the midst of it like we are. Thus he identifies with how we feel about our weakness and waywardness since he knows from the inside what it tastes like.

> For we do not have a high priest who is unable to sympathise with our weaknesses, but we have one who in every respect has been tested as we are, yet without sin. (Heb 4:15)

At the third level of his acceptance of us, Jesus asks us to see the limited and wayward side of ourselves in perspective, to see it as only a small part of the very good person we are. We find Jesus doing this in the way he highlights the goodness of the woman who washed his feet in Simon's house. Most of the other guests saw only her sinfulness and would have rejected her as 'a bad woman', not worthy to be there.

> Then turning toward the woman, he said to Simon, 'Do you see this woman? I entered your house; you gave me no water for my feet, but she has bathed my feet with her tears and dried them with her hair. You gave me no kiss, but from the time I came in she has not stopped kissing my feet. You did not anoint my head with oil, but she has anointed my feet with ointment. Therefore, I tell you, her sins, which were many,

have been forgiven; hence she has shown great love. But the one to whom little is forgiven, loves little.' (Luke 7:44-47)

At the fourth level we see how, in spite of all our weakness and waywardness, and even in some mysterious way because of them, we are rejoiced over and delighted in by Jesus. He reveals this in three parables he tells in chapter 15 of Luke's gospel that are pervaded by joy. In the parable of the lost sheep we find there, we have a symbol of the way Jesus seeks out the parts of ourselves we have lost touch with or have 'put away' because we are ashamed of them. He delights in and even celebrates this limited or sinful side of us, for where we are weakest is very often where we are most heroic. There are aspects of ourselves we may be ashamed of or frustrated with that Jesus admires in us, as they are the areas of our lives where over the years we have struggled heroically to improve.

Now all the tax collectors and sinners were coming near to listen to him. And the Pharisees and the scribes were grumbling and saying, 'This fellow welcomes sinners and eats with them.' So he told them this parable: 'Which one of you, having a hundred sheep and losing one of them, does not leave the ninety-nine in the wilderness and go after the one that is lost until he finds it? When he has found it, he lays it on his shoulders and rejoices. And when he comes home, he calls together his friends and neighbours, saying to them, "Rejoice with me, for I have found my sheep that was lost." Just so, I tell you, there will be more joy in heaven over one sinner who repents than over ninety-nine righteous persons who need no repentance.' (Lk 15:1-7)

We have an illustration of these different levels of Jesus' acceptance of our limitations and sinfulness in Luke's description of what happened on the road to Emmaus. (Lk 24:13-36) There we find Jesus joining two of his disciples who had deserted him when he needed them most. He is content not only to accompany them in their troubled state but gives them the opportunity to talk out their troubles and to have these listened to sympatheti-

cally. With the help of the Word he then puts their experience in
perspective by helping them to see it in the light of the whole
story of his love for them. But it is in the light of their experience
of Jesus in 'the breaking of the bread' that they realise that in
spite of all their limitations they are loved 'to the utmost extent'.
It is in our ongoing experience of the Mass or 'the breaking of the
bread' that we too continue to experience Jesus' desire to recon-
cile us to himself in all these ways.

The Mass and reconciliation

To conclude this chapter we will reflect briefly on how our longing for reconciliation and Jesus' desire to satisfy this longing is
reflected in the prayers of the Mass. Built into the Mass is a
movement towards making our relationships increasingly inclusive that we may 'be brought together in unity by the Holy
Spirit'.

> May all of us who share in the body and blood of Christ
> be brought together in unity by the Holy Spirit.
> *(Eucharistic Prayer II)*

Being forgiven and being reconciled with God and others is an
essential part of the central prayer of the Christian, the Our
Father.

> and forgive us our trespasses
> as we forgive those who trespass against us;

At Mass we pray that the beauty of God's constant forgiveness
of our sins may inspire us to extend this forgiveness to all we
meet.

> Father of our Lord Jesus Christ,
> in your unbounded mercy
> you have revealed the beauty of your power
> through your constant forgiveness of our sins.
> May the power of this love be in our hearts
> to bring your pardon and your kingdom to all we meet.
> *(Opening Prayer of Week XXVI)*

Some suggestions for reflection and prayer

1. Read the following story and in a few words express what it highlights for you. For example, what does it highlight about guilt, forgiveness and reconciliation?

> *The Straight Story* is a film about two brothers who have been estranged for many years. When Alvin hears his brother has had a stroke, and he realises that he himself is not in good health, he decides to visit his brother so that they may be reconciled. The trouble is that they live hundreds of miles away from each other. Since Alvin does not drive a car and wants to make the journey alone, he decides to go on his sit-up lawnmower. The journey is eventful in an inner as well as in an outer way as Alvin comes to terms with his personal limitations and those of the people he meets on his journey. He gradually realises how difficult he has found dealing with his intolerance of his own limitations and those of others. As a result of this self-acceptance, the people he meets on his journey put him in touch with the wiser and gentler person in him that seeks to be reconciled with his world. Six weeks and several breakdowns later he arrives at his destination. As he sits with his brother in the verandah of his house they are silent for some time. Then his brother looks at the lawnmower and remarks, 'You came all this way on that just to see me!'

2. Tell the story of a mistake you made that you find it hard to forget and to forgive yourself for. How do you feel as you recall this incident? If you find that you have held on to feelings like sadness, guilt or resentment, ask yourself what way would you suggest to a friend to deal with such feelings he or she tends to hold on to?

3. Spend some time quietening yourself and then focus in on what troubles you most at present. Jesus joins you and asks you to share with him how you feel. He listens sensitively and sympathetically until you have said all you want to. Let him not only

accept but even identify with you in your weakness and temptations. Then, let him highlight a healthy way you have handled
the areas of weakness that you have shared with him. Finally,
dwell with one thing he says to you and then tell him how you
feel about this.

4. Prayerfully reflect on the story of Jesus appearing to two disciples on the road to Emmaus. (Lk 24) You may find it helpful to
focus on one or more of the following verses: 17, 27 and 30-32.
You may want to reflect on the following four references and how
they focus in on four ways Jesus accepts you and wants you to accept yourself: (Mt 13:28-30, Heb 4:14-15, Lk 7:36-50, Lk 15:3-7).

PART 5

'That you may be completely one'

In Part 4 we examined how the Mass transforms us, drawing us into an intimate union with Jesus, with each other and with everything in our environment. In Part 5 we will examine the nature of this union and some of the qualities it has that are highlighted in the communion of the Mass.

Chapter 17 reflects on three aspects of the Mass as a meal that are highlighted in the communion prayers. There is the love that invites us to the meal, the close bond it renews and the joy that surrounds it.

Chapter 18 looks at how communion provides a space in which we can savour the vision of Jesus' glory, or of the radiance of his love, which we are given at Mass.

Chapter 19 dwells on the nature of the union that the vision of Jesus' glory, or the beauty of his love, draws us into.

Chapter 20 describes how the love we experience at communion and the union it draws us into is the source of a profound joy.

Babette's Feast

The story of the film, *Babette's Feast,* centres on a famous French chef called Babette who was forced to go into exile for political reasons. In the small village in Denmark where she settles down there is a Christian community held together by the two daughters of the pastor who had formed the community. When Babette arrives the pastor has been dead for a number of years so that his powerful influence on the community has waned. His two daughters, who have agreed to employ Babette as their cook, strive to maintain their father's influence but they are not able to exert the kind of influence he did and so the community has become fragmented.

Babette's work, however, is not confined to cooking for the two sisters. Encouraged by them, she begins to look after various members of the aged village community who have been neglected and have as a result become isolated and disgruntled. Though at first they are reluctant to accept her help, they grow to welcome her visits and as a result of her quiet charm their spirits are raised and they are drawn back into the community again.

Some time after her arrival in the village, Babette wins 10,000 francs in the French lottery and she decides to spend it on a feast for the whole village. In this feast the profound nature of Babette's care is demonstrated by the fact that she spends all her money on the meal, but even more so by the artistry with which she prepares this superb meal. Her ultimate goal, however, as it had always been at the Café Anglaise in Paris, was to make people happy. For her, preparing this meal was primarily the art of caring for people by nurturing their body and delighting their spirit.

CHAPTER 17

The communion highlights the Mass as a meal

In this chapter we reflect on a number of aspects of the meal that are emphasised in the communion of the Mass.

The feast

The story of the film, *Babette's Feast,* is built around a wonderful meal. In providing it Babette spends all the money she has and brings to its preparation all her artistry as one of the finest chefs in France. All this trouble she went to was to give the small community of the village where she lived an experience of happiness. But more importantly she gave them an experience of a spectacular act of kindness which must have remained in their memory as a source of inspiration for the rest of their lives. It must have been for them a moment when love became radiant, a moment of great joy of being together again as a community when they had all but fallen apart.

A family get-together

I am one of 11 children. Though we do not often get together as a family, we enjoy the times when we do. There have been rifts in the relationships between various members of the family in the past as there had been in my father's family. It is, therefore, understandable that when he was dying my father gathered the family around him and appealed to us to stick together. He believed that apart from the bond with God, the family bond was the most basic one and it was his dying wish that we should do anything that was necessary to preserve it.

We have taken his wish seriously and while we believe in living our own lives and having 'gaps in our togetherness', we take the pains to remain in contact. Our concern for each other becomes very tangible when any of us is ill or goes through dark times. Over the years, the highlight of our being together has been the occasional meal we meet for. The fact that some member of the family hosts this and undertakes all the organisation involved says something important to us.

As well as the experience of the love that draws us together and the joy of meeting, a strong sense of the bond between us is renewed and this remains tangible long after our get-together. There is something about this bond between us that is basic to our holding environment. I now realise that it was within my family that I learned the most basic things about this environment during my most formative years. Perhaps, what was most significant for me during those years of growing up together was the meals we shared. Those were the most intimate moments of our day when we had time to relate, to talk and to enjoy each other's company. Meals were also an experience of the very tangible love of our parents, providing food for us and preparing it.

A threefold blessing

In recent years, three aspects of the meals we get together for are striking. There is first of all *the love that gathers us together*. This is most obvious in those who organise our getting together. Meals also *build up and renew a bond* between us, as they provide a much needed space to relax, to sit together and to share what is going on for us. This time we take out to listen and talk to each other does more than anything else to build up and maintain the bond between us. Meals are also a time when *we enjoy ourselves*. This joy is helped by the pleasure of a good meal but its main source is found in the experience of being together.

The role meals play in the Bible

There is a conviction often expressed in the Bible that it is dangerous to forget. This is especially true of our tendency to forget the good people we have met and the valuable experiences we have had along the way. When we forget these people and experiences, we cut ourselves off from what William Wordsworth calls that best portion of our lives, 'the little, nameless, unremembered acts of kindness and of love'. It is the awareness of these that sustains us by building up a loving environment against the constant erosion of it. Forgetting becomes most damaging when it means that we get cut off from the memory of the wonderful things God has done for us and from the 'kindness' these reveal.

> ... by sinking into deep forgetfulness they get cut off from your kindness. (Ws 16:11)

In the rituals the Bible developed to keep in touch with the 'kindness' of God, meals play a key role. It was through the Passover meal that the Israelites kept in touch with the Exodus which was the greatest event of the Old Testament. In the Passover meal they remembered the leaving of Egypt, crossing the Red Sea, journeying through the desert and the manna God gave them as food for their journey. It was in the memory of these wonderful works that they discovered how rich and varied was God's love. It was the constantly renewed experience of this love that made them more joyful than any of the peoples who surrounded them. It is this joy that is such a striking feature of the Psalms where God is described as clothing people with joy.

> You have turned my mourning into dancing; you have taken off my sackcloth and clothed me with joy, so that my soul may praise you and not be silent. O Lord my God, I will give thanks to you forever. (Ps 30:11-12)

Manna that sustains us on our journey
A major feature of the Exodus was the manna people were given to sustain them on this journey across the desert. It was provided on a daily basis and it was not be stored but to be collected each morning. As such it was a daily vision of 'the glory of the Lord', a daily reminder of the radiance of the love of God who sustained them, body and soul.

Then the Lord said to Moses, 'I am going to rain bread from heaven for you, and each day the people shall go out and gather enough for that day.' ... So Moses and Aaron said to all the Israelites, 'In the evening you shall know that it was the Lord who brought you out of the land of Egypt, and in the morning you shall see the glory of the Lord.' (Ex 16:4-7)

The food we ARE a hunger for

What Jesus comes to provide is often spoken of in the gospels in terms of a banquet or a wedding feast. At this feast Jesus is the bridegroom and we the bride. The food at this feast is the passionate love of God that Jesus embodies or is a revelation of. It is a food that *we are a hunger for*. Therefore, it is a matter of the greatest urgency that we come to the banquet and an utter mystery why we do not.

The kingdom of heaven may be compared to a king who gave a wedding banquet for his son. He sent his slaves to call those who had been invited to the wedding banquet, but they would not come. Again he sent other slaves, saying, 'Tell those who have been invited: Look, I have prepared my dinner, my oxen and my fat calves have been slaughtered, and everything is ready; come to the wedding banquet.' (Mt 22:2-4)

The messianic banquet

The story of the feeding of the multitude is told in all four gospels and there are two accounts of it in Matthew, Mark and Luke's gospels. The reason for this concentration of interest is that those who wrote the gospels see this event as a fulfilment of the messianic banquet. All the accounts of the feeding of the multitude also see it as a foretaste of the Mass since the words used to describe what Jesus did with the bread are similar to those he used when he gave us the Mass.

Jesus took the seven loaves, and after giving thanks he broke them and gave them to his disciples to distribute. (Mk 8:6)

It is John, however, who makes explicit the profound signifi-

cance that is referred to in the other three gospels. John hears
Jesus referring to 'the bread of life' as both the Word of God and
the body and blood of Jesus.

As is true of all the miracles Jesus worked, the feeding of the
multitude is a sign of God's love. However, here Jesus adds a
profound dimension to this love in that the bread he gives us is
his body and blood and as such is the supreme expression of his
love. But as well as being a sign of God's love, the feeding of the
multitude is a sign of God's providence or of a plan God is
working out in Jesus. It is a plan that we should become one
with Jesus as he wishes to become one with us.

Those who eat my flesh and drink my blood abide in me, and
I in them. Just as the living Father sent me, and I live because
of the Father, so whoever eats me will live because of me. (Jn
6:56-57)

Jesus promises that this bread he gives us will satisfy our most
basic hunger. This is the hunger *we are* to experience first hand
and to believe in the passionate nature of his love for us.

I am the bread of life. Whoever comes to me will never be
hungry, and whoever believes in me will never be thirsty. (Jn
6:35)

Three invitations
There are three things Jesus invites us to do in the following
words.

Take this, all of you, and eat it:
this is my body which will be given up for you.

Take this, all of you, and drink from it:
this is the cup of my blood,
the blood of the new and everlasting covenant.
It will be shed for you and for all men
so that sins may be forgiven.
Do this in memory of me.
(The Lord's Supper: the Consecration)

Firstly, these words invite us to remember his death and the love that inspired it. This love is expressed in his body 'given up' for us and in his blood 'shed for' us and there is none greater.

> No one has greater love than this, to lay down one's life for one's friends. (Jn 15:13)

Secondly, the words with which Jesus invites us to remember this ultimate expression of his love, invite us to 'eat' and 'drink', to savour and assimilate it. The effect of this is that in assimilating his love we are assimilated into him in a way that means we 'become completely one' with him in the way he is with his Father.

> ... that they may be one, as we are one, I in them and you in me, that they may become completely one. (Jn 17:22-23)

The third invitation of the Mass is that we enter Jesus' joy. This joy comes from the growing conviction that we are loved to the degree that Jesus' body 'given up' for us expresses in such a powerful way. Jesus says that he reveals this love so that we might share his joy in all its fullness.

> I have said these things to you so that my joy may be in you, and that your joy may be complete. (Jn 15:11)

In the following three verses from Chapter 15 of John's gospel we have an expression of the three features of the Mass as a meal that we will focus on in the final part of this book.

> As the Father has loved me, so I have loved you; abide in my love. If you keep my commandments, you will abide in my love, just as I have kept my Father's commandments and abide in his love. I have said these things to you so that my joy may be in you, and that your joy may be complete. (Jn 15:9-11)

Many of the prayers of the Mass emphasise the fact that it is a meal and none more so than the words at the centre of the Mass.

> When supper was ended,
> he took the cup.
> Again he gave you thanks and praise,
> gave the cup to his disciples, and said,
> Take this, all of you, and drink from it:

This meal is a banquet, the messianic banquet characterised by abundance. The following prayer lists some of the blessings that are part of this abundance.

> In this great sacrament you feed your people
> and strengthen them in holiness,
> so that the family of mankind
> may come to walk in the light of faith,
> in one communion of love.
> We come then to this wonderful sacrament
> to be fed at your table
> and grow into the likeness of the risen Christ.
> *(Preface of the Holy Eucharist II)*

In taking away our sins the Lamb of God takes away what separates us from others, the barriers to intimacy:

> This is the lamb of God
> who takes away the sins of the world.
> Happy are those who are called to his supper.
> *(Rite of Communion)*

The vision of his love Jesus keeps before us through the Mass is a joyful one.

> Source of life and goodness, you have created all things,
> to fill your creatures with every blessing
> and lead all men to the joyful vision of your light.
> *(Preface of Eucharist Prayer IV)*

Some suggestions for reflection and prayer

1. After reading again the story about *Babette's Feast*, notice how the following three themes are emphasised:

> The spectacular nature of her kindness,
> the unifying effect of this
> and the joy people experience in this.

2. Tell the story of a meal you invited others to or which you were invited to and focus especially on,

> The act of kindness that it was,
> how it drew people together, renewing the bond

between them
and how it was characterised by joy.

3. Be in your inner room for some time and let Jesus join you
there. All the blessings of your life are represented around the
walls of this room. After renewing a sense of how blest you have
been, Jesus asks you whether you see your life as a feast or a
famine, or as something in between. Before you part, say to Jesus,
'There is one thing I really want to say to you and it is this ....'

4. Reflect prayerfully on any of the following pieces of scripture
in the light of what has struck you in 1-3 above: Ex 16:16-18, Ps
23, Jn 6, Mt 22:2-9, Lk 22:14-20.

CHAPTER 18

'I have given them the glory you gave me'

In this chapter we will look at the strikingly beautiful vision of Jesus' love we are asked to contemplate in the communion of the Mass.

The emergence of Babette's beauty

The story of *Babette's Feast* is of a meal but even more so of the beauty of a person's act of kindness in providing and preparing it. The beauty of Babette's way of relating is even more striking than the kindness of the pastor who originally established the community. He appears in a number of the film's flashbacks and there is always a quiet radiance about the images of him we are given. On reflection we may also associate this same quiet radiance with Babette. This radiance is seen in the artistry or in the unobtrusive beauty of the way she relates with everybody in the village, no matter what their circumstances or mood may be.

The role of beauty

'I wonder whether we make sufficient use of beauty as the doorway leading to God.' So writes Cardinal Danneels as he compares the hold which truth, goodness and beauty have on the modern mind. As gateways to God, truth and goodness attract us. Beauty, however, disarms us; it has a powerful attraction for young and old alike. So Danneels concludes, 'Beauty can achieve a synthesis between truth and goodness. Truth, beauty and goodness: they are three of God's names and three paths that lead to him. But beauty has hardly been pressed into use by theology or religious teaching up until now. Isn't it time we do so?'

When I read these words of Cardinal Danneels I immediately identified with them. This is probably because the Christian vision has of late become for me not just true and good but beautiful too. As a student I was struck by the lack of attractiveness of the truth presented to us in philosophy and theology. The way it was presented in philosophy was divorced from life and in theology the truth appeared dogmatic and drab. Goodness too, as presented in theology, was negative in its approach to life, favouring as it did a correction rather than an affirmation model of growth. The creed and code of the institutional church I lived in at that time were not attractive or affirming as they were more an expression of 'good advice' than 'good news'. For example, when I read the parable of the good Samaritan I was taught to look for its meaning and its implications for my life. Generally, I found myself deficient in the way I measured up to the standard of behaviour the parable put before me. It was only later, when I learned to see the story as a picture of Jesus and of the intensely practical nature of the love he has for me, that the story became affirming rather than corrective. As a result of this experience the gospel stories began to paint for me a portrait of Jesus as a loving person. His attractiveness or beauty grew until I became enthralled by him.

Seeing Jesus' glory

Hans Urs von Balthasar has been called 'the greatest theologian of our era, and maybe of all time'. (Henri de Lubac) It is his conviction that we have lost a sense of the beauty of Christ and Christianity that people had in the first millennium. It was to reclaim this beauty that he wrote the seven volumes of his main work, *The Glory of the Lord.*

For Jesus, glory is based on the radiance or the beauty of the love he and his Father share. Thus the glory that Jesus speaks about is not an abstract idea but something made visible in the many aspects of the love he reveals. These aspects of his love are like the facets of a diamond, each of which reflects the diamond's beauty in a different way. For example, at the beginning of

John's gospel this glory is found in two aspects of Jesus' love
that are referred to as 'grace and truth':

> And the Word became flesh and lived among us, and we
> have seen his glory, the glory as of a father's only son, full of
> grace and truth. (Jn 1:14)

The 'grace and truth' mentioned here refer to the loving-kind
and faithful love that emerged from people's experience of God
in the Exodus. There God was found to be 'merciful and gracious', 'abounding in steadfast love and faithfulness'.

> The Lord ... a God merciful and gracious, slow to anger, and
> abounding in steadfast love and faithfulness, keeping stead-
> fast love for the thousandth generation, forgiving iniquity
> and transgression and sin. (Ex 34:6-7)

But the glory of God is also found in each gospel story. For example, we see it in Jesus' act of unobtrusive courtesy at the wedding feast at Cana.

> Jesus did this, the first of his signs, in Cana of Galilee, and re-
> vealed his glory; and his disciples believed in him. (Jn 2;11)

A more dramatic picture of Jesus' glory is presented in the trans-
figuration which anticipates the splendour of his resurrection.
At this turning point of the gospels, Jesus' glory is seen in the
spectacular nature of his love which inspired him to begin the
journey to Jerusalem and to his death.

> Now about eight days after these sayings Jesus took with
> him Peter and John and James, and went up on the mountain
> to pray. And while he was praying, *the appearance of his face
> changed, and his clothes became dazzling white.* Suddenly they
> saw two men, Moses and Elijah, talking to him. *They appeared
> in glory and were speaking of his departure, which he was about to
> accomplish at Jerusalem.* Now Peter and his companions were
> weighed down with sleep; but since they had stayed awake,
> *they saw his glory* and the two men who stood with him. (Lk
> 9:28-32)

The emergence of Jesus' glory

During his public life the glory of Jesus emerges in each gospel story. For example, people are struck by the 'gracious' way he relates. (Lk 4:22) The word gracious means merciful, benign, kind and courteous. We see this graciousness in the way Jesus *acknowledges* Zacchaeus' dignity, (Lk 19:1-6) *accepts* his weaknesses, (Lk 19:7-8) *appreciates* his basic goodness (Lk 19:9) and in the way Jesus is *concerned* for the welfare of one who was seen by others as an outcast. (Lk 19:10)

The Book of Glory

In chapters 13-21 of John's gospel we get a picture of the extent and depth of Jesus' glory. This section of his gospel is called 'the book of glory' because it is at this point in the Bible that the glory or the radiance of God's love reaches its climax in the extent, depth and intensity of Jesus' love. In the words of John, it is in Jesus' death and resurrection that we experience the ultimate expression of Jesus' love, that he loves us 'to the end' or 'to the utmost extent'. (Jn 13:1) Jesus himself speaks of his death as the greatest sign he could give of his love. (Jn 15:13) It is here in the radiance or beauty of his love that Jesus finds his Father's glory and his own. It is his 'hour' or the high point of his life.

Father, the hour has come; glorify your Son so that the Son may glorify you. (Jn 17:1)

Captivating people with his beauty

In four places in John's gospel we see the way the glory of Jesus 'arrests' people, how the splendour and beauty of his love captivates them. We see the *intensity* of Jesus' love, (Jn 13:1) how it *enthrals* people so that he becomes the centre of their lives (Jn 12:32) and *engages their whole person*. (Jn 12:19) As a result, their lives are *transformed*. (Jn 11:49-52)

In the resurrection scenes, and especially in John's commentary on these in chapters 13-17 of his gospel, we see how pervasive, enduring and profound Jesus' love is and the glory it radiates. We see how beautiful the enduring love of Jesus is in the way he accepts Peter back and draws him into an even more profound relationship than before. (Jn 21:15-19) How profound this relationship can become is revealed to us in the friendship Jesus calls us into. There has never been such a profound understanding of friendship and its beauty as that which Jesus wants to establish with each of us. For him friendship is a sharing not just of everything he has, but of all that he is, in complete self-disclosure.

> I have called you friends, because I have made known to you everything that I have heard from my Father. (Jn 15:15)

In inviting us to be his friends, Jesus opens up to us the most profound area of his life, his intimate relationship with his Father in all its glory. Friendship, however, calls for a mutual sharing and if we do answer this call by 'abiding in' their love, it leads to a joy that is as complete as it is constant.

> As the Father has loved me, so I have loved you; abide in my love. ... I have said these things to you so that my joy may be in you, and that your joy may be complete. (Jn 15:9-11) ... I will see you again, and your hearts will rejoice, and no one will take your joy from you. (Jn 16:22)

Our share in his glory

Jesus would not say that he loves us in the same way as his Father loves him without our being this lovable. This fact is echoed in one the prefaces of the Mass when it says that God sees and loves in us what he sees and loves in Jesus. *(Preface of Sundays VII)* If we are loved to this degree, we share in Jesus' glory or in the radiance of the love that Jesus and his Father find in us.

> The glory that you have given me I have given them. (Jn 17:22)

In reminding us that we are loved 'to the utmost extent', the Mass seeks to keep us in touch with the reality that we, like Mary, are 'radiant in beauty'.

Full of grace, she was to be a worthy mother of your Son,
your sign of favour to the Church at its beginning,
and the promise of its perfection as the bride of Christ,
radiant in beauty.
... and our pattern of holiness.
(Preface of the Immaculate Conception)

To make this beauty more real for us, scripture compares it to
that which God as the bridegroom finds in each of us as his
bride. (Is 62:2-5) Paul uses this image of the husband and wife to
illustrate the love Jesus has for us when 'he sacrificed himself'
for us to make us 'altogether glorious' in his eyes. (Eph 5:25-32)

When we eat the body of Christ and drink his blood in the
communion of the Mass we are asked to savour and to take in a
stunningly beautiful reality. This is the fact that by assimilating
Christ's love, and our own resulting lovableness, we are trans-
figured like Jesus was on Mount Tabor. We are, in Paul' words,
'transfigured in ever-increasing splendour' or 'transformed
from one degree of glory to another' into the likeness of Jesus.
This glory is a reality that we need to repeatedly taste and
savour in the quiet time we make for ourselves in the communion of the Mass.

But all of us Christians have no veils on our faces, but reflect
like mirrors the glory of the Lord. We are transfigured in
ever-increasing splendour into his own image, and the transformation comes from the Lord who is the Spirit. (2 Cor 3:18,
J. B. Phillips)

'We are God's work of art'

Because we share God's glory and reflect its radiance, we are
more than anything else in creation 'God's work of art'. (Eph
2:10) The foundation for this role is laid in our being made in
God's image. (Gen 1:27) As a result we have the capacity to receive and return God's love and this means that we share and reflect God's glory and become God's work of art in two intimately
connected ways. The first of these ways results from the fact that

we are now true images of Jesus or 'conformed to his image in order that he might be the firstborn within a large family'. (Rom 8:29) This transformation is an ongoing one so that 'we are trans-figured in ever-increasing splendour' into the image of Jesus. As a result, 'we reflect like mirrors the glory of the Lord' (2 Cor 3:18) in the way the following prayer says we do.

Father,
let the gift of your life
continue to grow in us,
drawing us from death to faith, hope and love.
Keep us alive in Christ Jesus.
Keep us watchful in prayer
and true to his teaching
till your glory is revealed in us.
(*Opening Prayer of Week XVI*)

This vision of our glory or beauty that Jesus puts before us at Mass has a powerful effect on the way we relate with others. The more we recognise in ourselves the beauty that God finds in us, the more we are inclined to recognise it in others too. Nothing urges us to treat others graciously as having this high estimation of them. We become clearer and more assured not only about doing what is right, fair and just but we develop an artist's sense for what is just right. Under the inspiration of the Spirit's gift of Counsel we are led to know instinctively the 'more excellent way' or the art of loving that for Paul surpasses all other forms of art. (1 Cor 12:31-13:4-8) This artistry with which we relate with others in developing the art of loving is the second way we are God's work of art.

An all-pervading glory

The more aware we become of how we all share Jesus' glory, the more aware we become of how each part of creation, no matter how small, can put us in touch with this glory. The glory with-out triggers off the awareness of the glory within and sends us back to its source. This view of everything in our environment as a wayside sacrament means, that 'the world is charged with the

grandeur of God'. (G. M. Hopkins) We can say Jacob's words
not only of every person we meet but of every place and circum-
stance we find ourselves in: 'How awesome is this place! This is
none other than the house of God, and this is the gate of heaven.'
(Gen 28:10-17) We recognise the truth of Hopkins' words:
      ... Christ plays in ten thousand places,
      Lovely in eyes, lovely in limbs, not his. (G. M. Hopkins)

Some suggestions for reflection and prayer
1. What does the story and the quotation below say to you about
the glory that lies hidden in each of us? Does the story say anything to you about how you might arouse this sense of the glory
or beauty of your life?

   Who do you believe?
   The film, *Calender Girls*, tells the story of twelve middle-aged
   women who produce a calendar to support a charitable
   cause. Each of the twelve poses partially nude for a photo-
   graph that represents a particular month. The venture transforms them, for by taking part in it each of them becomes
   aware of her own distinctive beauty and that of the others.
   Their experience is epitomised in the words of one husband
   who says of his wife, 'I have watched the various stages of
   the growth of your beauty, but this present stage is the most
   glorious of all.'

   Truth, beauty and goodness: they are three of God's names
   and three paths that lead to him. But beauty has hardly been
   pressed into use by theology or religious teaching up until
   now. Isn't it time we do so?
   (Cardinal Danneels)

2. Tell the story of a person who stands out for you in the way he
or she relates. Name one thing that strikes you about the way
this person relates or loves. Does he or she give you a sense of
your own goodness? How do you feel in his or her presence?

3. After being quiet for a short while, dwell with an incident in which someone loved you in a striking way. See can you find the exact words to express what this person said to you in effect in this incident. Savour these words to let their attractiveness grow on you. Finally, let Jesus say them to you a number of times and tell him how you feel about him saying them to you.

4. Reflect prayerfully on any of the following pieces of God's Word: Jn 1:14, 2:11, 17:22, 2 Cor 3:18.

CHAPTER 19

'That they may be one as we are one'

In this chapter we reflect on how the glory or beauty of Jesus' love draws us into a union with him, with ourselves, with others and with all things that Jesus says is 'complete'.

Reuniting the community

In bringing the elderly people a meal each day, and with the courtesy with which she does this, Babette draws them out of their isolation and back into the community again. This bridge Babette has been building between people is finally put in place when she invites them to the feast she has prepared for them. What is remarkable about the way she reunites the community is that prior to her coming all had centred around the pastor as the one who held the community together. Now it is Babette who fulfils this same role even though she always remains in the background. It is interesting that she hardly appears during the feast but remains in the kitchen and continues the work of drawing them together from there.

Four levels of intimacy

In the early 1980s I was introduced to the Myers Briggs system of discerning types of temperament. What appealed to me about it most was that it introduced me to the four levels at which we relate and the contribution each makes to intimacy. For example, when we remember the details of our story there is the intimacy the body and its five senses offer us at the sensate level at which we relate. There is an intimacy that emerges at the feeling level when we share how we feel about what has happened to us in our story. Then there is the intimacy that emerges at the in-

tuitive level when we take the time to notice the insights into another's goodness that the significant events of our story offer us.
Finally, at the convictional level a deep and permanent intimacy
opens up when we dwell with our convictions of being loved
and of being loving. Realising the contribution that each of these
levels of experience makes to intimacy has been one of the most
fruitful discoveries of my life.

From my own experience and from what I see happening in
the lives of others, I have noticed a distinct pattern in the way we
move from one of these four levels at which we relate to another.
At the beginning of a relationship closeness or intimacy is often
judged in terms of the sensate and feeling levels at which we experience it. With time the intuitive and convictional levels can
become the source of a deeper and more permanent intimacy.
This happens when we learn to notice and to express the
glimpses of another's goodness which we are given, and when
we learn too how to treasure and appropriate these glimpses so
that they become convictions or part of what we believe about
another. From sharing these convictions, a union of mind and
heart can come about. This union does not discard the sensate
and feeling levels at which we relate but depends on them to
keep it earthed, affectionate and warm.

A love as strong as death
There is a point in the *Song of Songs* when the woman, who is
telling the story of the love of her life, reflects on how this love
has developed. She reflects on what has happened between herself and her beloved, on the range of emotions that have swayed
her this way and that, on the insights she has gathered and on
the convictions she has come to. What strikes her most about the
wisdom life has taught her is the power of love as the driving
force behind all her experience. It is this love which has drawn
her to the one she loves and has involved her whole person,
senses, soul, heart and mind in the growth of this relationship.
She realises that initially she thought she could control love and
use it for her own purposes to possess her beloved physically

and to dictate to her feelings. But she gradually realises that love has its own way of involving our whole person in the way we relate and it will not be diverted from this.

> Set me as a seal upon your heart,
> as a seal upon your arm;
> for love is strong as death,
> passion fierce as the grave.
> Its flashes are flashes of fire,
> a raging flame.
> Many waters cannot quench love,
> neither can floods drown it.
> If one offered for love
> all the wealth of his house,
> it would be utterly scorned.
> (Song of Songs 8:6-7)

The intimacy or union Jesus draws us into
It is this power of love to unite and even make us 'completely one' with himself and his Father that Jesus wants to work with.

> ... that they may be one, as we are one, I in them and you in me, that they may become completely one. (Jn 17:22-23)

Rather than analysing the nature of the union Jesus draws us into, we may learn more about it from reflecting on how Jesus entices us into it. He does this right from the beginning of the gospel story. For example, in chapter 1 of John's gospel we see Jesus calling two young people to come and get to know him.

> When Jesus turned and saw them following, he said to them, 'What are you looking for?' They said to him, 'Rabbi' (which translated means Teacher), 'where are you staying?' He said to them, 'Come and see.' They came and saw where he was staying, and they remained with him that day. It was about four o'clock in the afternoon. (Jn 1:38-39)

It is interesting to notice that Jesus calls 'those whom he wants' first of all 'to be with him' as his companions and only then does he send them out. The primary call is to fellowship. The call to be generative comes after the call to intimacy and is always dependent on it.

> He went up the mountain and called to him those whom he wanted, and they came to him. And he appointed twelve, whom he also named apostles, to be with him, and to be sent out to proclaim the message. (Mk 3:13-14)

As well as calling us to be with him as his companions Jesus calls us by our name. A name in the Bible is a symbol of a unique relationship and when Jesus calls each of us by name it is into this unique relationship with him.

> The gatekeeper opens the gate for him, and the sheep hear his voice. He calls his own sheep by name and leads them out. When he has brought out all his own, he goes ahead of them, and the sheep follow him because they know his voice. (Jn 10:3-4)

A growing attractiveness

By calling us by name, or in a deeply personal way, Jesus becomes increasingly attractive to us as he did to his first disciples. An indication of how attractive he tends to become is the fact that all else became secondary for his first disciples soon after they met him. They 'left everything' in order to be with him.

> When they had brought their boats to shore, they left everything and followed him. (Lk 5:11)

Jesus expresses the power of his attractiveness in the parable of the pearl of great price. The way people sell all to possess it symbolises how we can become so attracted by Jesus that we leave all else aside in order to be with him.

> Again, the kingdom of heaven is like a merchant in search of fine pearls; on finding one pearl of great value, he went and sold all that he had and bought it. (Mt 13:45-46)

A time came in Paul's life, as it does in varying degrees in the life of every Christian, when Jesus became so attractive and central that all else was relatively unimportant compared to being with him.

I regard everything as loss because of the surpassing value of
knowing Christ Jesus my Lord. For his sake I have suffered
the loss of all things, and I regard them as rubbish, in order
that I may gain Christ and be found in him, not having a
righteousness of my own that comes from the law, but one
that comes through faith in Christ, the righteousness from
God based on faith. I want to know Christ and the power of
his resurrection and the sharing of his sufferings by becoming like him in his death. (Phil 3:8-10)

What climaxes Jesus' attractiveness for John and enthrals him is
the death and resurrection of Jesus. John sees the love that these
events reveal as what draws us to Jesus like a powerful magnetic
force.

And I, when I am lifted up from the earth, will draw all people to myself. (Jn 12:32)

It is this love, which inspired the death of Jesus, which we are
asked to 'eat' and 'drink', or to remember, to savour and to assimilate at Mass. The effect of this is that we don't just assimilate
Jesus' love but that we are assimilated by it and so live in him as
he lives in us.

Those who eat my flesh and drink my blood abide in me, and
I in them. (Jn 6:56)

Images of the union Jesus wants with us
Jesus uses a number of images to help us grasp the nature of this
union in which he lives in us and we in him. What these images
are chosen to convey is the astounding reality that we are drawn
into the life that Jesus, his Father and their Spirit share. Jesus
uses the image of the vine and its branches to illustrate how this
union is based on our sharing a common source of life. (Jn 15:4-
5) The effect of this sharing is that they will make their home
with us.

Those who love me will keep my word, and my Father will
love them, and we will come to them and make our home
with them. (Jn 14:23)

A very powerful image of this union is used by Paul when he compares it to that which exists between the parts of our body.

For just as the body is one and has many members, and all the members of the body, though many, are one body, so it is with Christ. For in the one Spirit we were all baptised into one body – Jews or Greeks, slaves or free – and we were all made to drink of one Spirit. (1 Cor 12:12-13)

All these images are meant to give us a glimpse of an intimate relationship that is so close that it becomes a union that Jesus says is the same as the complete union that exists between him, his Father and their Spirit.

... that they may be one, as we are one, I in them and you in me, that they may become completely one. (Jn 17:22-23)

This union Jesus draws us into is the ultimate expression of the holding environment we seek to renew at Mass. As we saw in the introduction to this book, this environment is a place where we feel secure, cared for, significant, accepted and affirmed. As we saw in Part, 4 it is Jesus' desire that all our relationships should become part of this environment, our relationships with significant people, with ourselves, with others and with everything in creation.

It is hard to be realistic about Jesus' call to be 'completely one' as he and his Father are one, unless we work out in practical terms how this union takes shape. We need to ask ourselves, How do we become close to, intimate and even one with another person? To suggest an answer to this question we will look at three things on which this closeness, intimacy or union depends.

1. WHAT is shared

What we share with others, or open up of ourselves to them, can be compared to four windows that open onto our inner world. Opening the first costs us very little for what is inside is the most general information about ourselves that we would reveal to anyone. When we open the second window we reveal the more personal details of our story. These are not for everybody's ears but their revelation is necessary if we are to reveal to them something meaningful about ourselves. The third window opens onto experiences that we tell few people about. This may be because we do not pay much attention to these experiences or it may be because we are reluctant to share this intimate or personal side of ourselves. We open the fourth window to nobody as we hardly know what is behind it and if we do, it is for our eyes only.

We saw in Part 1 and 2 that Jesus wants to share 'everything' he has and is with us and especially the intense love that he has for his Father and for the Spirit. In chapters 14 to 17 of John's gospel Jesus tells us about three aspects of this love that he wants to share with us. He wants to share his glory or the radiance of his love as well as the joy and the union the intense attractiveness of his love draws us into. In sharing 'everything' with us Jesus creates a bond, an intimacy, a union that he calls friendship.

> I have called you friends, because I have made known to you everything that I have heard from my Father. (Jn 15:15)

2. HOW this is shared

Our intimacy or union with others depends on how we share with them, whether it is at a sensate, feeling, intuitive or convictional level. At the sensate level we become close to others when we tell them our story, especially its more significant events. Our feelings are aroused when we remember these events and if we take the trouble to share these feelings it leads to a new level of intimacy. The reason why events arouse strong feelings is that they are saying something important to us, they give us glimpses of ourselves and others. If we can put words on these and then share them with someone we take a major step to becoming intimate with that person. If we stay with these glimpses we can gradually convert them into convictions about what is true and what we value most about ourselves and others. If we take the trouble to arouse this deepest level of our experience and share even a small part of our vision and what we value most, a union of mind and heart emerges.

When Jesus tells us about the most intimate reality in his life, the love he and his Father share with their Spirit, he invites us to 'abide in' this love. He tells us this involves immersing our whole person in their love by receiving and returning it with 'our whole heart, soul, mind and strength'.

> What must I do to inherit eternal life? ... You shall love the Lord your God with all your heart, and with all your soul, and with all your strength, and with all your mind ... Do this, and you will live. (Lk 10:25-28)

3. The QUALITY of the sharing

Our closeness to people depends a lot on our capacity to listen and to respond to them and they to us. In other words, our relationships are governed by the principle that they are as good as the communication going on within them. We see how Jesus worked on the basis of this principle when he told us that those who want to be intimate with him must listen and respond to his self-revelation in the word of God.

> Then his mother and his brothers came to him, but they could not reach him because of the crowd. And he was told, 'Your mother and your brothers are standing outside, wanting to see you.' But he said to them, 'My mother and my brothers are those who hear the word of God and do it.' (Lk 8:19-21)

The union we pray for at Mass

Many of the prayers of the Mass are an expression of our desire to be close to, intimate and one with God. One of the prayers of the Mass expresses the belief that Jesus comes among us 'to lift up all things to himself, to restore unity to creation'. (Jn 12:32)

> He has come to lift up all things to himself,
>
> to restore unity to creation,
>
> and to lead us from exile into your heavenly kingdom.
>
> *(Preface of Christmas II)*

It is especially through his body and blood that our union with Jesus and his Spirit is nourished so that we become one body, one spirit.

Grant that we, who are nourished by his body and blood,
may be filled with his Holy Spirit
and become one body, one spirit in Christ.
(Eucharistic Prayer III)

Ultimately it is the passionate love of Jesus symbolised by his body 'given up' for us and his blood 'shed' for us that helps us 'to live as one family the gospel we profess'. (Jn 11:52)

God our Father,
we rejoice in the faith that draws us together,
aware that selfishness can drive us apart.
Let your encouragement be our constant strength.
Keep us one in the love that has sealed our lives,
help us to live as one family
the gospel we profess.
(Opening Prayer of Week XI)

Some suggestions for reflection and prayer

1. How intimate with or close to you do you allow others to become? Examine three relationships, one with someone you work with, a second with a family member and a third with a close friend and reflect on how the closeness or intimacy of these three relationships differs.

2. Recall some of the main events that mark the development of a close relationship you enjoy. In the light of this relationship, does Jesus' desire to be 'completely one' with you (Jn 17:23) make much sense?

3. In your imagination enter a dialogue with the person you are closest to. Talk about the kind of intimacy you enjoy with each other or about the kind you would like to have.

4. Reflect prayerfully on the kind of intimacy Jesus would like with you and you would like with him in the light of any of the following: Jn 11:52, 12:19, 12:32, Lk 8:19-21, Jn 17:22.

CHAPTER 20

A joy that is constant and complete

In this chapter we will examine how the Mass is a celebration, how the love Jesus reveals to us at Mass and the intimacy with him which this draws us into, is a source of deep and lasting joy.

A celebration of life

The meals Babette brought to people gave them great pleasure but even more so the quiet courtesy with which she brought them. Before her coming, many in this elderly community felt neglected and were saddened by their isolation. In her attentiveness to them, Babette restored their sense of being included in the community again and their joy in this. She saw herself as an artist and the purpose of her art to bring joy to people's lives, to help them celebrate life in spite of all its shortcomings. We can see how, as the feast she prepared progressed, the pleasure of good food and wine had its way with these people. This is in spite of the fact that they came to the feast with the resolve that they would drink the wine only to avoid offending Babette. When this normally subdued group of people actually came to the feast, an atmosphere of celebration enveloped them. In the light of their change of mood to one of joy it seems natural that the film should end with their celebration of life as they dance around the village well in the middle of the night.

More concern than celebration

I grew up on a farm during the years immediately after the Second World War. Even though they were years of scarcity, we fared better than a lot of people as the farm produced most of the basic kinds of food that we needed. There were certain

drawbacks, however, to living on a farm as there was an unend-
ing series of jobs to be done. As a result, I associated my holidays
from school with work on the farm as this occupied most of my
day. I envied my friends whose holidays seemed to be much
more carefree, much more about play than work. However,
when I look back from my present perspective, I realise that because of having to work so hard on the farm, my leisure time
though limited was all the more treasured. Because leisure was
so scarce I learned to relish and to make the most of it. At the
time, however, it was work, rather than leisure and enjoyment,
that was central to my life.

When I left school and went to the seminary this philosophy
of hard work prevailed. We were trained for work with little attention given to how we spent our leisure time. The kind of
Christianity that prevailed was of a serious and even sombre
sort, the emphasis being more on the cross in Jesus' life and in
our own than on the resurrection and the joy associated with it.
It was as if the joy of the next life had to be earned by the way we
bore the suffering and sadness of this life.

The true place of leisure and its joy

I was in my late twenties when I came across a book called,
Leisure the Basis of Culture by a German philosopher called
Joseph Pieper. It was he who introduced me to and opened up
the possibilities of Aristotle's belief that:

We are active to be leisurely

rather than leisurely to be active.

This realisation was like a seed that was sown in an inhospitable
soil and that thus took a long time to germinate and to mature.
However, it opened up the possibility that leisure and the joy essential to it are at the heart of the Christian faith and its fullness
need not be postponed until the next life. It was only in the middle of my years that I was led to see that *we are made for joy* and
that this joy is the purpose of God's self-disclosure in Jesus. I
began to realise that the true basis of Christian joy is to be found
in the words of Jesus when, after revealing how much he loves
us and how we can abide in this love, says:

'I have told you these things that you might share my joy and that your happiness may be complete.' (Jn 15:9-11)

This joy that Jesus wants in all its completeness for us pervades the whole Bible but especially the infancy narratives, the resurrection scenes, and it characterises the lives of the early Christians in the Acts of the Apostles.

If we are to take what Jesus says about joy seriously, we need to ask ourselves questions like the following: 'In the gospel story, do I see Jesus as a happy person? Does joy have an important place in his teaching? Is it at the heart of the gospels or somewhere off-centre or even peripheral? How much of his joy do I allow him to share with me? Is happiness an inside job in the sense that it depends on a choice I am called to make or does it depend largely on outer circumstances?'

The source of our joy
The Mass seeks to cultivate an environment in which joy pervades. It does this by renewing our vision of what is this joy's deepest source. This is our belief that we are loved by Jesus in the same way that he is loved by his Father.

As the Father has loved me, so I have loved you; abide in my love ... I have said these things to you so that my joy may be in you, and that your joy may be complete. (Jn 15:9-11)

There is nowhere in the Bible that joy is spoken of more profoundly than in these verses. In them Jesus says that the ultimate source of our joy is in 'abiding' or immersing ourselves in his love. In practice, 'abiding in' Jesus' love means getting our whole person, 'heart, soul, mind and strength' involved in it. From each of these four levels at which we relate a distinctive joy emerges. There is a joy that is proper to the sensate and the feeling ways we relate as there is to the intuitive and convictional ways. Even though 'the supreme happiness comes from the conviction of being loved' (Victor Hugo) all the other levels have their distinctive contribution to make to our joy.

A joy that is complete

It is hard for us to believe that Jesus wants our happiness more than we do our own. That he would want this happiness to be perfect, abundant or without limit may seem unrealistic and therefore be resisted as too good to be true. It is strange that we resist the happiness Jesus offers us for we not only crave happiness but are made for it. We not only long for happiness as one among many other human longings but *we are this longing, this hunger.*

The reason we resist the happiness Jesus offers is probably because what is on offer within our daily experience is usually so limited that we have learned to make do with a happiness that is only a fraction of what Jesus offers us. We may feel that this limited version is all we have a right to expect if we are to be realistic. However, this limitation of our joy is not based on the vision Jesus opens up for us at Mass. This is a vision of ourselves as loved 'to the utmost extent' and Jesus promises us that if we abide in it our happiness will be 'complete'. (Jn 15:9-11)

A joy that is constant

Jesus also highlights the fact that the joy he wants for us is as unlimited in its extent as it is in its depth. Whereas the joy we earn by our own efforts is fragile and fleeting, that which Jesus offers us is as robust and constant as his love is. If joy comes from faith in the fact that we are loved, then the Mass, as the constant reminder that we are loved 'to the end', is our greatest assurance that the joy Jesus offers is an enduring one.

> When a woman is in labour, she has pain, because her hour has come. But when her child is born, she no longer remembers the anguish because of the joy of having brought a human being into the world. So you have pain now; but I will see you again, and your hearts will rejoice, and no one will take your joy from you. (Jn 16:21-23)

What erodes our joy

If we are to enter into the complete and constant joy Jesus offers us at Mass, it is necessary to be aware of the ways we resist it. What causes most resistance is the image of God we live with. For example, in the film *Babette's Feast*, the people Babette comes to live among seemed to live with an image of a very serious and sombre God. The impression we get is that their God would not approve of them enjoying the wine Babette had ordered for the feast. Similarly, the image of Jesus we live with may not be of a joyful person, not even as joyful as many people we know who have a healthy sense of leisure and enjoyment. Our image of a serious and zealous Jesus, and our consequent lack of awareness of joy in the gospel stories, can make it difficult for us to take seriously Jesus' desire that our joy might be complete and constant.

Our resistance to the complete and constant joy Jesus offers us may also be based on the misconception that it is unrealistic to expect a high level of joy in life. This may be because we have been led to see life from the point of view of the cross and the large amount of suffering that is part of each person's story. Seen from this angle, the joy of the resurrection is greatly diminished or perhaps understood as belonging mainly to the next life. When we say Psalm 22 we may tend to identify more with 'the valley of darkness' than with 'the banquet', the 'overflowing cup' and 'the goodness and kindness' with which God leads us. (Hos 11:3-4) Again, the Hail Holy Queen, that has been one of our most popular prayers, paints a grim picture of us 'poor banished children of Eve, weeping and wailing in this valley of tears'.

Our sense of joy may also be eroded by our tendency, for personal, historical or religious reasons, to identify more with the valley periods of life than with its peak periods. In this context the resurrection and its all-pervasive beauty and joy may appear too good to be true. Our sense of joy can also be eroded by the climate of excessive consumerism that prevails today. Because we are so driven by concern for what we might have we often justify the postponement of enjoying what we already have to some future time.

'All the way to heaven is heaven.'
> Earth's crammed with heaven,
> And every common bush afire with God.
> But only he who sees takes off his shoes,
> The rest sit around it and pluck blackberries.

From a Christian point of view, Elizabeth Barrett Browning's be-belief that 'Earth's crammed with heaven' is not only beautiful but realistic. It is in keeping with St Catherine of Sienna's belief that 'all the way to heaven is heaven'. What these two women be-lieved is especially true if our main focus in life is on the resur-rection and the joy essential to it. This belief that 'peace and joy' are of the essence of 'the kingdom of God' is also central to Paul's picture of the Christian life.

> For the kingdom of God is not food and drink but righteous-ness and peace and joy in the Holy Spirit. (Rom 14:17)

'Happiness is an inside job'

We are tempted to believe that joy depends on circumstances, that it is a matter of chance rather than choice, of fate rather than of faith. But joy is ultimately a matter of who and what we choose to believe, whether we elect to listen to the word of God and obey it or not. This is the recipe for happiness that Jesus of-fers us in the Word and in the Mass as the climax of what the Word reveals.

> While he was saying this, a woman in the crowd raised her voice and said to him, 'Happy the womb that bore you and the breasts that nursed you!' But he said, 'Happier still are those who hear the word of God and obey it!' (Lk 11:27-28)

The saying that 'Happiness is an inside job' is based on the fact that our happiness is rooted in our choice to believe or not to be-lieve what is revealed to us at Mass. We are tempted to believe that our lives do not amount to much rather than to believe that we are utterly lovable and worthwhile as the Mass so powerfully says we are. We readily pick up messages about our insignifi-cance and that we are inadequate or do not measure up to people's expectations. We are inclined to ruminate on these and to identify with them. The 10% that is deficient catches our eye, holds our attention and adds another chapter to the history of our deficiency. This 10% becomes more real and tangible than the 90% of us that the Mass offers us a vision of. This is a vision of ourselves as immeasurably significant and worthwhile.

Cultivating a joyful environment

The environment Jesus wants us to live in is one where a constant and complete joy prevails. This kind of joy is based on the conviction that *faith* makes us capable of developing, the conviction that we are loved by Jesus just as he is by his Father. (Jn 15:9-11, 16:21-22) As well as this joy that springs from faith in Jesus' *love* there is also a profound joy that *hope* inspires. This is what is called in the prayers of the Mass a 'joyful hope' and it is based on the plan and the promise of Jesus to lead us through his Spirit 'into all the truth', (Jn 16:13) into the full extent and depth of his love that may yet be ours. (Eph 3:14-21) Paul tells us that 'we can be full of joy here and now even in our trials and troubles' as these produce 'a steady hope, a hope that will not disappoint us'. (Rom 5:3-5)

What faith, hope and love open up for us is a caring environment characterised by joy. This environment is the space we cultivate in which the Father, Jesus and the Spirit reveal themselves to us and in which they share with us the 'complete joy' this revelation brings with it. The joy that characterised the environment in which God invited the people of the Old Testament to live becomes the complete and constant joy that characterises the environment Jesus wants us to live in.

I speak these things in the world so that they may have my joy made complete in themselves. (Jn 17:13)

The Mass as a celebration

The word peace is often used for joy or happiness in the prayers of the Mass. In the Jerusalem Bible peace is described as 'the perfect happiness and deliverance which the Messiah would bring'.

It is this meaning of the word peace that the communion prayers refer to when, for example, we pray for 'the peace and unity' of the church and to Jesus as the Lamb of God to 'grant us peace'. In one of the communion prayers inspired by the promise of Jesus to share his own peace with us, (Jn 14:27) we pray:

Lord Jesus Christ, you said to your apostles:
I leave you peace, my peace I give you.
Look not on our sins, but on the faith of your Church,
and grant us the peace and unity of your kingdom
where you live for ever and ever.
(Rite of Communion)

The prayers of the Mass depict it as a celebration, as a time when 'we celebrate the memory of Christ', especially of the love that inspired his passion, resurrection and ascension into glory.

Father, we celebrate the memory of Christ, your Son.
We, your people and your ministers,
recall his passion,
his resurrection from the dead,
and his ascension into glory.
(Eucharistic Prayer I)

In other prayers the Mass is spoken of as a 'joyful vision', and as the source of 'every blessing'.

Father in heaven,
it is right that we should give you thanks and glory;
you alone are God, living and true.
Through all eternity you live in unapproachable light.
Source of life and goodness, you have created all things,
to fill your creatures with every blessing
and lead all men to the joyful vision of your light.
(Preface of Eucharistic Prayer IV)

Some suggestions for reflection and prayer

1. What is your reaction to the saying that we are made for joy? Would the Jesus you know believe in this? Enter the following fantasy and see are you comfortable with the image of Jesus it will invite you to be with.

> Imagine that Jesus invites you to go for a walk. You welcome this as you have a number of problems you want to get his advice on. The only difficulty you foresee is that Jesus seems to be in one of his lighthearted moods today but you feel you may be able to work him around to take what you want to discuss seriously. You are just ready to introduce your first problem when he points out some flowers he is very excited about. You let him be with this for some time for you know there is no stopping him in his enthusiasm. After trying a few more times and being foiled by other interests of his, you decide to join Jesus in his lighthearted mood.

2. List a few areas of your life where you find joy. In which of these do you find most joy? Is there a fun-loving side of you that needs to find time to play? Tell the story of the side of you which believes that we are made for joy, the side of you that can be lighthearted and leisurely. This is the side of you that is convinced that you need to enjoy the simple abundance of the present moment.

3. Is there a side of you that believes there is something suspicious about cultivating a culture of enjoyment and that a culture of concern is much more in keeping with our Christian belief? Remember an incident in the story of this side of you that lives within a culture of concern or that believes we are leisurely to be active. Then enter a dialogue with the side of you that would like to live in a culture of enjoyment or that believes we are active to be leisurely.

4. Reflect prayerfully on any of the following pieces of scripture in the light of what has arisen for you in 1-3 above: Jer 29:11-14, Jn 15:11, 16:19-22.